MIDDLE GRADES MATHEMATICS PROJECT

Probability

Elizabeth Phillips

Glenda Lappan

Mary Jean Winter

William Fitzgerald

Addison-Wesley Publishing Company

Menlo Park, California • Reading, Massachusetts • Don Mills, Ontario
Wokingham, England • Amsterdam • Sydney • Singapore
Tokyo • Mexico City • Bogotá • Santiago • San Juan

Acknowledgments

"Fair and Unfair Games I" and ideas for the area models from *Teaching Statistics and Probability* in the NCTM Yearbook 1981. Reprinted by permission of the National Council of Teachers of Mathematics.

"Prof says lottery drawing not fair" by Keith Gave. *Lansing State Journal*, January 17, 1982, p. 19. Abridged and reprinted by permission of Lansing (Mich.) State Journal.

This book is published by the Addison-Wesley Innovative Division.

ISBN 0-201-21478-4

13 14 15 - ML - 95 94

About the authors

William Fitzgerald, Ph.D. in mathematics education, University of Michigan, joined the faculty of Michigan State University in 1966 and has been Professor of Mathematics and Education since 1971. He has had extensive experience at all levels of mathematics teaching and has been involved in the development of mathematics laboratories.

Glenda Lappan, B.A., Mercer University, Macon, Georgia, and Ed.D., University of Georgia, is Professor of Mathematics at Michigan State University. She directed the mathematics component of MSU Sloan Foundation Minority Engineering Project. She has taught high school mathematics and since 1976 has worked regularly with students and teachers of grades 3–8.

Elizabeth Phillips, B.S. in mathematics and chemistry, Wisconsin State University, and M.S. in mathematics, University of Notre Dame, was visiting scholar in mathematics education at Cambridge University, England. She conducts inservice workshops for teachers and is the author of several papers and books. Currently she is a faculty member in the Department of Mathematics at Michigan State University.

Janet Shroyer, B.S., Knox College, and Ph.D., Michigan State University, has taught mathematics in Lansing public schools and at Oregon College of Education. She was a consultant in the Office of Research Services, evaluator of a teacher corps project, and a research intern in the Institute for Research on Teaching. Presently she is Associate Professor in the Mathematics Department of Aquinas College, Grand Rapids, Michigan.

Mary Jean Winter, A.B., Vassar College, and Ph.D. in mathematics, Carnegie Institute of Technology, has been Professor of Mathematics at Michigan State University since 1965. She has been involved in mathematics education at both school and college (teacher training) level since 1975. She has been especially interested in developing middle school and secondary activities using computers and other manipulatives.

A special note of recognition

Sincere appreciation is expressed to the following persons for their significant contribution to the Middle Grades Mathematics Project.

Assistants:	**David Ben-Haim** **Alex Friedlander** **Zaccheaus Oguntebi** **Patricia Yarbrough**
Consultant for evaluation:	**Richard Shumway**
Consultants for development:	**Keith Hamann** **John Wagner**

Contents

Probability

The Middle Grades Mathematics Project (MGMP) is a curriculum program developed at Michigan State University funded by the National Science Foundation to develop units of high quality mathematics instruction for grades 5 through 8. Each unit

- is based on a related collection of important mathematical ideas
- provides a carefully sequenced set of activities that leads to an understanding of the mathematical challenges
- helps the teacher foster a problem-solving atmosphere in the classroom
- uses concrete manipulatives where appropriate to help provide the transition from concrete to abstract thinking
- utilizes an instructional model that consists of three phases: launch, explore, and summarize
- provides a carefully developed instructional guide for the teacher
- requires two to three weeks of instructional time

The goal of the MGMP materials is to help students develop a deep, lasting understanding of the mathematical concepts and strategies studied. Rather than attempting to break the curriculum into small bits to be learned in isolation from each other, MGMP materials concentrate on a cluster of important ideas and the relationships that exist among these ideas. Where possible the ideas are embodied in concrete models to assist students in moving from the concrete stage to more abstract reasoning.

THE INSTRUCTIONAL MODEL: LAUNCH, EXPLORE, AND SUMMARIZE

Many of the activities in the MGMP are built around a specific mathematical challenge. The instructional model used in all five units focuses on helping students solve the mathematical challenge. The instruction is divided into three phases.

During the first phase the teacher *launches* the challenge. The launching consists of introducing new concepts, clarifying definitions, reviewing old concepts, and issuing the challenge.

The second phase of instruction is the class *exploration*. During exploration, students work individually or in small groups. Students may be gathering data, sharing ideas, looking for patterns, making conjectures, or developing other types of problem-solving strategies. It is inevitable that students will exhibit variation in progress. The teacher's role during exploration is to move about the classroom, observing individual performances and encouraging on-task behavior. The teacher urges students to persevere in seeking a solution to the challenge. The teacher does this by asking appropriate questions and by providing confirmation and redirection where needed. For the more able students, the teacher provides extra challenges related to the ideas being studied. The extent to which students require attention will vary, as will the nature of attention they need, but the teacher's continued presence and interest in what they are doing is critical.

When most of the students have gathered sufficient data, they return to a whole class mode (often beginning the next day) for the final phase of instruction, *summarizing*. Here the teacher has an opportunity to demonstrate ways to organize data so that patterns and related rules become more obvious. Discussing the strategies used by students helps the teacher to guide them in refining these strategies into efficient, effective problem-solving techniques.

The teacher plays a central role in this instructional model. The teacher provides and motivates the challenge and then joins the students in exploring the problem. The teacher asks appropriate questions, encouraging and redirecting where needed. Finally, through the summary, the teacher helps students to deepen their understanding of both the mathematical ideas involved in the challenge and the strategies used to solve it.

To aid the teacher in using the instructional model, a detailed instructional guide is provided for each activity. The preliminary pages contain a rationale; an overview of the main ideas; goals for the students; and a list of materials and worksheets. Then a script is provided to help the teacher teach each phase of the instructional model. Each page of the script is divided into three columns:

TEACHER ACTION	TEACHER TALK	EXPECTED RESPONSE
This column includes materials used, what to display on the overhead, when to explain a concept, when to ask a question, etc.	This column includes important questions and explanations that are needed to develop understandings and problem-solving skills, etc.	This column includes correct responses as well as frequent incorrect responses and suggestions for handling them.

Worksheet answers, when appropriate, and review problem answers are provided at the end of each unit; and for each unit test, an answer key and a blackline master answer sheet is included.

RATIONALE

"Probability theory is the underpinning of the modern world. Current research in both the physical and social sciences cannot be understood without it. Today's politics, tomorrow's weather, and next week's satellite all depend on it."

How to Take a Chance
Darell Huff and Irving Geis

Probability plays an increasingly important role in our daily lives. In addition to its use in games of chance, it is also used to make decisions in such diverse fields as scientific research, weather forecasting, military operations, business predictions, insurance calculations, design and quality control of consumer products, politics, heredity, and social science.

Introduction

Probability is fun for students. Using experiments and games to teach probability concepts provides an enjoyable experience for all students—even those who have not previously experienced success in mathematics. The basic ideas are accessible to all students, yet the richness of the subject easily provides extra challenges for students.

Probability promotes systematic, logical thinking. Students are continually making hypotheses and supporting conclusions. The process of generating hypotheses and testing them experimentally and theoretically is a useful and necessary tool for analysis of statistical arguments and for making informal decisions.

Probability is a useful tool to illustrate and deduce many mathematical ideas. It is pertinent to the middle grades because it provides a sound understanding of the concept of fractions, including equivalent fractions and comparison of fractions. By using the area model to analyze dependent events, a solid basis is formed for addition and multiplication of fractions. The unit provides practice with whole number operations and with decimals and percents for older students.

UNIT OVERVIEW

An integral part of the pedagogy of this unit is the use of manipulatives in experiments. That is, students guess at the outcome of a situation and then test their conjectures by experimenting (playing the game). This is followed by analytically comparing the experimental and theoretical results. Throughout the unit students should be encouraged to make notes on the concepts and strategies developed. These can be made on activity sheets so that students have a complete record of what they learned.

The ten activities in this unit fall into three natural groups. The unit can be taught as a whole, or each group can be used separately.

Group I: Fair and Unfair Games—Activities 1–4 and the Computer Activities

These activities provide the basic definitions of probability and methods of conducting an experiment and of determining experimental probabilities. They also provide the tools for systematically analyzing and determining theoretical probabilities such as listing, tree diagrams, and charts. Computer Activity III is an interesting excursion into the use of computers and probabilities. Histograms are used to display probabilities, and the knowledge gained in the first three activities is used to play and analyze games.

Group II: Expected Value—Activities 6, 7, 8

The area model for analyzing dependent events is introduced. The other new idea is that of expected value. The expected value, or expectation, is the average payoff (points, money, etc.) over the long run.

Group III: Binomial Probabilities—Activities 9 and 10

This is a concentrated look at probabilities in which there are only two equally likely outcomes: heads-tails, odd-even, boy-girl, win-lose, true-false, etc. It concludes with a derivation of Pascal's Triangle and how to use it to compute binomial probabilities.

Activity 5 involves an application of probability—that of conducting a survey and using the results to make decisions. The activity could be used at any time after the basic ideas of probability have been studied.

Activity 1 STATE LOTTERY

OVERVIEW

In this activity, students are introduced to the basic notions of probability and its uses in everyday life. A definition of probability and the use of the words *fair* and *unfair* to describe probability situations that have a game-like aspect are developed from two activities. Both activities are whole group, teacher-directed activities. The first involves drawing colored blocks from a bag. The second is a simulation of the Michigan State Lottery Three-Aces game.

The definition of probability is introduced in the beginning by a whole class discussion focusing on drawing colored blocks out of a bag: "If we reach into the bag and draw out a single block, what is the probability that it will be blue?"

$$\text{Probability of drawing a blue block} = \frac{\text{the number of blue blocks}}{\text{the total number of blocks}}$$

In more general terms, we think of an event as the *result* of a draw, a throw, a roll, etc., and the probability (P) that a particular result (A) will occur is

$$P(A) = \frac{\text{the number of ways A can occur}}{\text{the total number of possible results}}$$

P(A) is a convenient notation for "the probability of event A happening." By changing the number and color of blocks in the bag, the definition and significance of probabilities equal to 0 or 1 can also be established. In each drawing situation, the probabilities of all possible events are added and found to be 1. Consequently, $P(A) + P(\text{not } A) = 1$ provides a strategy for solving some of the problems on Worksheet 1-1.

Students are introduced to the idea of *fair* and *unfair* situations by simulating the drawing of a winning number in a state (Michigan) lottery. Students are assigned one of the two digit numbers 10 through 34: 3 ping pong balls numbered 1, 2, and 3 are put into a bag. 10 Ping Pong balls numbered 0–9 are put in a second bag.

The first digit of the two-digit number is determined by drawing a ball from the first bag. The second digit is determined by drawing a ball from the second bag. If a 3 is drawn first, then the balls are drawn and *replaced* in the second bag until one of the digits 0, 1, 2, 3, or 4 are drawn. Fifteen to twenty simulations are enough to show students that this method of drawing favors numbers 30–34. By the end of this activity, students should begin to have a healthy scepticism for situations involving probability (chance).

Note: Probability is defined as a fraction. Thus, to compare probabilities equivalent fractions are used. For example, if $P(A) = \frac{1}{3}$ and $P(B) = \frac{1}{2}$, P(A) is less than P(B) since $\frac{1}{3} = \frac{2}{6}$ and $\frac{1}{2} = \frac{3}{6}$ and $\frac{2}{6} < \frac{3}{6}$. For older students decimals or percents or both can be used to express probabilities. This might make it easier to compare probabilities.

Activity 1

Goals for students

1. Understand the definition of probability.
2. Understand that a probability of 0 describes an event that is impossible.
3. Understand that a probability of 1 describes an event that is a certainty.
4. Understand that in a given situation the sum of the probabilities of all possible outcomes is 1.
5. Simulate a situation and discuss the results.
6. Understand the definitions of fair and unfair as applied to games or probabilistic situations.
7. Use probability to decide whether a situation (or event) is fair or unfair.

Materials

One set of three–six colored blocks (or chips, marbles, balls) of three different colors.

Two large paper bags (or suitable containers for drawing).

Ping Pong balls: two numbered 1, two numbered 2, two numbered 3; one each numbered 0, 4, 5, 6, 7, 8, 9.

Play money in $1,000,000 amounts (Materials 1-1).

Newspaper article for display (Materials 1-2).

Worksheets

1-1, Blocks and Marbles.

STATE LOTTERY

TEACHER ACTION	TEACHER TALK	EXPECTED RESPONSE
Ask.	Have you ever heard the word *probability?* What does it mean?	Various answers; the chances something will or will not happen.
Discuss briefly, depending upon the students' previous knowledge.	Can you describe some situations that use probability?	Various answers: weather, sports, medicine, games, etc.
Place one blue block and one yellow block in a bag (or use marbles, chips, etc.).	If I ask a student to draw a block from the bag without looking, what color will the student draw? How many say yellow? Blue?	Most students will say you can't tell. It is 50-50, equally likely, same chance for each, etc.
Have a student draw. Show class the color and put it back.	If we draw again what color will be drawn?	Students will say it is equally likely for each.
Repeat this two or three more times. Ask class to vote each time on what color they think will come up next.		
Ask.	Why did you vote this way?	If the same colored block is drawn several times in a row, some students may claim this color is more likely to be drawn or that the other color is now bound to come up next. Allow students to discuss this occurrence.
Tell.	The chance of drawing a yellow block does not depend on what happened on the previous trials. That is, blocks do not remember. Each block always has the same chance of being drawn.	

TEACHER ACTION	TEACHER TALK	EXPECTED RESPONSE
Tell.	In this bag containing one blue block and one yellow block the chance of drawing a blue is one out of two. The chance of drawing a yellow is one out of two, or 50-50. How can we express this as a fraction?	$\frac{1}{2}$
Define.	The probability of drawing a blue block is $\frac{\text{total number of blue blocks}}{\text{total number of blocks}} = \frac{1}{2}$	
Explain that we would like a shorter way of writing a probability statement.	We write $P(B) = \frac{1}{2}$ also $P(Y) = \frac{1}{2}$	
Add a blue block to the bag.	What is the probability of drawing a blue block?	$\frac{2}{3}$
	What is the probability of drawing a yellow block?	$\frac{1}{3}$
Take out the yellow block.	What is the probability of drawing a blue block?	$\frac{2}{2}$ or 1
	If an event has probability = 1, we say the chances of this event occurring is a *certainty*.	
	What is the probability of drawing a yellow block?	$\frac{0}{2}$ or 0
	If an event has probability = 0, the chances of this event occurring are *impossible*.	

TEACHER ACTION	TEACHER TALK	EXPECTED RESPONSE
Empty the bag and put one yellow, one blue, and one red block in it.	When we reach into the bag and draw out one block how many *different events* are possible?	Three; draw a yellow, draw a blue, or draw a red.
	What is the probability of drawing a red?	$P(R) = \frac{1}{3}$
	What is the probability of drawing a blue?	$P(B) = \frac{1}{3}$
	What is the probability of drawing a yellow?	$P(Y) = \frac{1}{3}$
	What is the *sum of the three probabilities?*	$\frac{1}{3} + \frac{1}{3} + \frac{1}{3} = \frac{3}{3} = 1$
Optional: Double the number of each color of blocks and find the probabilities. $PR(R) = \frac{2}{6}$ $P(B) = \frac{2}{6}$ $P(Y) = \frac{2}{6}$ Show that these probabilities (equivalent fractions) are the same as those for the preceding experiment		
Put another red block and two blue blocks into the bag.		
Ask and record.	How many blocks are in the bag?	Six.
	When we draw out one block how many different colors could it be?	Three: blue, red or yellow.
	How many ways could we draw a blue?	Three
	How many ways could we draw a red?	Two.
	How many ways could we draw a yellow?	One.

TEACHER ACTION	TEACHER TALK	EXPECTED RESPONSE
This would be a good place to mention equivalent fractions again:	Find the probability of drawing a red, P(R).	$P(R) = \frac{2}{6}$
$\frac{2}{6} = \frac{1}{3}, \frac{3}{6} = \frac{1}{2}$, etc.	Find P(B).	$P(B) = \frac{3}{6}$
	Find P(Y).	$P(Y) = \frac{1}{6}$
	Find the sum of the probabilities.	$\frac{2}{6} + \frac{3}{6} + \frac{1}{6} = \frac{6}{6} = 1$
Ask.	If a student computes the probability of drawing a red as $\frac{6}{5}$, is this possible?	No; $P(R) \leq 1$; the student inverted the fraction, counted wrong, etc.
	Why?	
Tell.	A probability will always be a fraction between 0 and 1, including 0 and 1.	
Put three blue blocks, two red blocks, and one yellow block in the bag.		
Ask.	How many blocks and of what kind must be added to make $P(Y) = \frac{1}{2}$?	Some students will answer two yellow blocks.
If a student answers two yellows, ask.	How many blocks are there all together?	8
	What is P(Y)?	$\frac{3}{8}$
	Remember that when we add yellow blocks the number of yellows changes, but so does the *total* number of blocks.	
	So how many blocks should we add? Why?	Four yellow blocks; $P(Y) = \frac{5}{10} = \frac{1}{2}$

TEACHER ACTION	TEACHER TALK	EXPECTED RESPONSE
	Now what is P(R)?	$P(R) = \frac{2}{10}$
	Now what is P(B)?	$P(B) = \frac{3}{10}$
		Some students may suggest in the beginning to add two yellow and take away two other blocks. Tell students we can only add, not take away blocks.
Review.	Find the P(R or B).	$\frac{2 + 3}{10} = \frac{5}{10}$ or $\frac{1}{2}$
	Find the sum: P(R) + P(Y) + P(B).	$\frac{2}{10} + \frac{5}{10} + \frac{3}{10} = \frac{10}{10}$ or 1
	What is P(not drawing a red)?	$1 - \frac{2}{10} = \frac{8}{10}$ or $\frac{5}{10} + \frac{3}{10} = \frac{8}{10}$ or (without addition) there are eight ways of not drawing a red, hence $P(\text{not } A) = \frac{8}{10}$
Tell the story of the Michigan Lottery. (See Materials 1-2.)	Many states have lotteries. The state of Michigan has a million-dollar lottery. All 11,561 of the winners of a $50 "Aces Three" game were assigned a number and invited to the million dollar drawing.	

TEACHER ACTION	TEACHER TALK	EXPECTED RESPONSE
	To determine the millionaire, the lottery bureau drew a single digit from each of the five pools corresponding to the place value positions until a five-digit number corresponding to one of the numbers 00001 to 11,561 was completed. If a number was drawn that did not fall in the range needed to complete the five-digit number, it was thrown back and another number was drawn.	
Ask.	Did each contestant have the same chance of winning the million dollars?	Various answers.
Explain. For a good simulation the number of students used should be either 14 or 24 or 34 depending on the size of your class. Use extra students or commissioners, drawers, etc. Assign a two-digit number 10–24, 10–34, or 10–44 as needed to each contestant. The important thing is that there be four or five possibilities in the last decade, the 20s or 30s or 40s depending on the size of your class. Otherwise it takes too many simulations for the problem to show up. We will illustrate with 10–34.	To help us answer the question we will act out, or *simulate,* the million dollar drawing with two-digit numbers because we only have ☐ students in our class. I will need a commissioner to hand out the money to the winners, and two people to draw. In the bag there are three Ping Pong balls each with a number 1, 2, or 3. In the second bag there are ten Ping Pong balls each with a number 0, 1, 2, 3, 4, 5, 6, 7, 8, or 9. We will draw out of the first bag to determine the tens digit and out of the second bag to determine the units digit. If the number drawn from the second bag does not complete a number in our range, we will replace the ping pong ball in the second bag and draw another units digit until we get a winner.	
Simulate the lottery drawing 15–20 times. (Materials 1-1)	We will do this several times. Our commissioner will give each winner a 1 million dollar bill.	

OBSERVATIONS	**POSSIBLE RESPONSES**		
	Record the numbers in this way:		
	tens		
	10 11, 11, 11 14	15	18
	twenties		
	20, 20 21, 23, 23	24 26, 26 27, 27	28
	thirties		
Students will begin to see the unfairness when after a 3 is drawn first, several draws are necessary to determine a 30s number.	30, 30 31 31 31 31 32 32 32 34		

TEACHER ACTION	TEACHER TALK	EXPECTED RESPONSE
Discuss the results of the lottery.	Do you think each contestant has an equal chance of winning?	Various answers. Most students will have observed that during the drawing, once a three was drawn, the people with a thirty number had more of a chance of winning.
	Raise your hand if you are still in the running if a 1 is drawn from the first bag.	Ten hands should be raised.
	So ten people would be competing for the prize.	
	What if a 2 is drawn from the first bag?	Ten hands should be raised.
	Again ten people would be competing for the prize.	
	What if a 3 is drawn from the first bag?	Five hands should be raised.
	Here only five people are competing for the prize!	
	What is the probability of drawing a 1, 2, or 3 from the first bag?	$\frac{1}{3}$
	If a 1 is drawn from the first bag, what is the probability of drawing 0, 1, 2, 3, 4, 5, 6, 7, 8, 9 from the second bag?	$\frac{1}{10}$
	If a 2 is drawn first, what is the probability of drawing a 0, 1, 2, 3, 4, 5, 6, 7, 8, or 9?	$\frac{1}{10}$

TEACHER ACTION	TEACHER TALK	EXPECTED RESPONSE
Ask.	If a 3 is drawn first, what numbers will we keep from the second bag?	Answer depends on class size; if the numbers 10–34 are used, the answer is 0, 1, 2, 3, or 4.
	What is the probability of a 0, 1, 2, 3, or 4 being drawn?	$\frac{1}{5}$
	Which contestants had a better chance of winning? Can you decide this on the first drawing?	Those with numbers 30–34; yes, if a 3 is drawn then the 30s have a better chance on the second draw.
	How could we make it fair?	Keep any number that is drawn from the second bag. If it does not correspond to a contestant's number, start all over again with the tens digit; put in the entire number for each contestant and draw out one number.
Tell.	The Michigan Lottery did change their drawing to make the probabilities equal for all contestants.	
Optional: Show students the article on the Michigan Lottery (Materials 1-2). Put it on the bulletin board. Worksheet 1-1, Blocks and Marbles, can be assigned as homework.	Ask students to bring in articles or descriptions of incidents where probability is used and make a bulletin board, collage, or book on probability in daily life.	

Materials 1-1

$1,000,000 DOLLARS	$1,000,000 DOLLARS
$1,000,000 DOLLARS	$1,000,000 DOLLARS
$1,000,000 DOLLARS	$1,000,000 DOLLARS
$1,000,000 DOLLARS	$1,000,000 DOLLARS

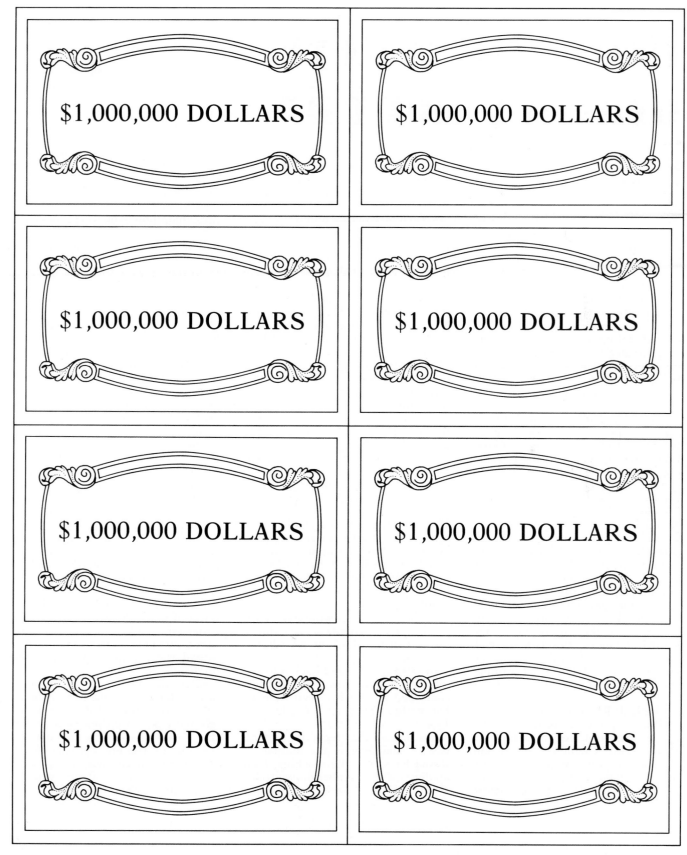

NATIONAL NEWS

Prof says lottery drawing not fair

By KEITH GAVE
Staff Writer

Not everyone has an equal chance of becoming a millionaire because the state lottery bureau uses an unfair procedure to select finalists for its million-dollar drawing, a Michigan State University professor of statistics and probability charges.

And if the system is not changed, a select few contestants could have an overwhelming advantage over the majority in a similar drawing among qualifiers—$50 winners—in the current instant lottery game, "Match Two," MSU's Martin Fox said.

FOX STUDIED the probability of certain five-digit numbers being selected from a pool of 11,561 combinations—which represent the number of possible contestants in the Dec. 30, 1981 drawing—which determined the five finalists for Thursday's million-dollar drawing in Flint's Hyatt Regency.

Fox said his analysis, based on procedures set by a Bureau of State Lottery directive concluded that not every $50 instant game winner who qualifies for the million-dollar drawing has the same chance of winning.

In the game "Aces Three" that began Sept. 9, there were 11,561 instant $50 winning tickets that could have qualified for the December elimination drawing to determine the finalists and several alternates.

BUREAU RULES require each $50 qualifier to file a form with the agency in order to collect a check for that amount. Accompanying the $50 check is a five-digit number assigned in chronological order to each contestant. In the Aces Three contest these numbers range from 00001 to 11,561. These are the numbers the qualifiers hold in the drawing which determine the five finalists.

According to Fox's findings:

—Those contestants assigned the five digit numbers 00001 through 00009 had a one in 18,000 probability of being selected as one of the five finalists.

—Those with numbers 00010 through 09999 had a one in 20,000 probability of being selected.

—Those with numbers 10000 through 10999 had a one in 4,000 probability of being selected.

—Those with numbers 11000 through 11499 had a one in 2,400 probability of being selected.

—Those with numbers 11500 through 11559 had a one in 1,680 probability of being selected.

—Contestants who were assigned the two remaining numbers, 11560 and 11561, had a one in 336 probability. "That's pretty good," Fox noted.

FOX, WHO has been with MSU for 22 years, took issue with the bureau's system of drawing numbers from a pool and returning to the pool those numbers that fall out of the range needed to complete the five-digit number.

In the Dec. 30 drawing, for example, the first two digits of one number were 11. If the third number drawn was a 6, 7, 8 or 9, it was considered "out of range," tossed back into the machine and redrawn. The process continued until a five-digit number fell within the range of 00001 to 11,561.

Fox argued that for absolute fairness, if one digit of the number is tossed back into the machine, then all digits of the number drawn so far should be tossed back. He admitted that getting five five-digit numbers using that system might be a lengthy and tedious process. Nevertheless, he said, before the first number even pops out of the bingo blower machine, each contestant would have an equal chance of becoming a finalist.

OBVIOUSLY, according to his conclusions, those who bought their $50 ticket and collected their winnings—and their number—earlier in the contest had a lesser chance of winning than those who were among the last to file.

Lottery officials noted, however, that only 11,067 of the 11,561 $50 instant tickets were sold. And of those, only 10,256 were claimed by contestants who were then mailed a five-digit number.

Fox said figuring the probabilities for those numbers would be "very complicated," without knowing exactly which numbers were missing from the range.

"But my guess, and it's only a guess, is that the gaps are roughly uniformly spread," he said, "which would preserve roughly the same unfairness."

FOX SAID his calculations were based on a bureau directive he called "well written and easier to understand than most government documents.

"If they mean what they're saying, then my opinion is correct and the procedure is very unfair to people (who are assigned) low numbers," he said.

Fox made his analysis at the request of Erwin R. Braker, one of the contestants in last month's elimination drawing and one of a handful to attend the ceremony to select the finalists.

After the first two digits were drawn (for each of the five finalists), Braker was eliminated. He said he left with an unsettling feeling that the process of selecting the numbers was biased. His number was 00400. He later inquired about the process to a lottery bureau official, who referred him to experts at MSU.

NAME

Blocks and Marbles

1. A box contains one blue block, one red block, and one yellow block.

a. What is the probability of drawing a blue block? P(B) = ____

What is the probability of drawing a yellow block? P(Y) = ____

What is the probability of drawing a red block? P(R) = ____

b. Find the sum of the probabilities in part a.

c. What is the probability of not drawing a blue block?
What is the probability of not drawing a yellow block?
What is the probability of not drawing a blue nor a yellow block?

2. A bag contains exactly three blocks, all blue.

a. What is the probability of drawing a blue block?

b. What is the probability of *not* drawing a blue block?

c. What is the probability of drawing a yellow block?

3. A bag contains two yellow marbles, four blue marbles and six red marbles.

a. What is the probability of drawing a yellow marble?

b. What is the probability of drawing a red marble?

c. What is the probability of drawing a blue marble?

d. What is the sum of the probabilities in parts a, b, and c?

e. What is the probability of *not* drawing a blue marble?

f. How many marbles must be added to the bag to make the probability of drawing a blue marble equal to $\frac{1}{2}$?

4. A bag contains some red, some white, and some blue marbles. The probability of drawing a red marble is $\frac{1}{3}$ and the probability of drawing a white marble is $\frac{1}{3}$. What is the probability of drawing a blue marble?

Brain Teasers

5. A bag contains several marbles. Some are red, some are white, and some are blue. The probability of drawing a red marble is $\frac{1}{6}$ and the probability of drawing a white marble is $\frac{1}{3}$.

a. What is the probability of drawing a blue marble?

b. What is the smallest number of marbles that could be in the bag?

c. Could the bag contain 48 marbles? If so, how many of each color?

d. If the bag contains four red marbles and eight white marbles, how many blue marbles does it contain?

[illegible] and Marbles

1. A box contains one blue block, one red block, and one yellow block.

   a. What is the probability of drawing a blue block? ____
   What is the probability of drawing a yellow block? ____
   What is the probability of drawing a red block? ____

   b. Find the sum of the probabilities in part a.

   c. What is the probability of not drawing a red block?
   What is the probability of not drawing a yellow block?
   What is the probability of not drawing a blue or a yellow block?

2. A box contains exactly three blocks [illegible]

   a. What is the probability of drawing a blue block?

   b. What is the probability of not drawing a blue block?

   c. What is the probability of drawing a yellow block?

3. A bag contains two yellow marbles, [illegible] and [illegible] marbles.

   a. What is the probability of drawing a yellow marble?

   b. What is the probability of drawing a red marble?

   c. What is the probability of drawing a blue marble?

   d. What is the sum of the probabilities in parts a–c?

   e. What [illegible] drawing a [illegible]?

   f. How [illegible] added to the bag [illegible] the probability of drawing a blue marble is [illegible]?

4. [illegible] contains some red, some white, and some blue marbles. The probability of drawing a red marble is [illegible] and the probability of drawing a white marble is [illegible]. What is the probability of drawing a blue marble?

[illegible]

A bag contains several marbles. Some are red, some are white, and some are blue. The probability of drawing a red marble is [illegible] and the probability of drawing a white marble is [illegible].

a. What is the probability of drawing a blue marble?

b. What is the smallest number of marbles that could be in the bag?

c. Could the bag contain [illegible] marbles? If so, how many of each color?

d. If the bag contains four red marbles and eight white marbles, how many blue marbles does it contain?

Activity 2

FAIR AND UNFAIR GAMES I

OVERVIEW

The story setting for this activity is that a toy manufacturer is considering marketing several new two-person games. The manufacturer would like to choose only fair games to market. The class is challenged to help the manufacturer make correct decisions about the games. Three games are analyzed: the first game involves two coins and is teacher directed. The next two games each involve three colored chips; the students work in pairs to play the games and determine the fairness of each.

The games are analyzed both experimentally and theoretically to determine fairness. This allows students to begin to see the effect of small samples of data versus larger samples and that theoretical probabilities reflect what happens in the long run (if the experiment is performed over and over). Coins and chips with each side lettered provide an easy introduction to experimentation-simulation. The theoretical analyses are easy since the number of outcomes is small. Making lists and simple tree diagrams help students learn a systematic way to determine the theoretical probabilities.

Finally, if a game is unfair, students are asked to show how to make it fair in two different ways—either by changing the points (payoff) or by changing the rules to change the probabilities.

Goals for students

1. Practice simulating situations.
2. Determine experimental probabilities.
3. Determine theoretical probabilities.
4. Organize data.
5. Analyze outcomes by listing.
6. Analyze outcomes by using a tree diagram.
7. Understand the definition of a fair game.

Materials

15 chips with both sides marked x.

15 chips with one side marked x and one side marked y.

15 chips with one side marked A and one side marked B.

15 chips with one side marked A and one side marked C.

15 chips with one side marked B and one side marked C.

30 pennies.

Paper cups for shaking chips (optional).

Worksheets

2-1, Chips.

2-2, More Chips.

FAIR AND UNFAIR GAMES I

TEACHER ACTION	TEACHER TALK	EXPECTED RESPONSE
Tell.	We have been asked by a game manufacturing company to test some new games they are considering. Some are simple, and some are more complex. We will be playing and analyzing the games. The company wants to know whether each game is fair for all players.	
Pose game.	In the first game, we will flip two coins: Player A gets 1 point if there is a match. Since there are two ways to get a match, we will give player B 2 points if there is no match.	
Ask. Get a show of hands. Make sure everyone votes.	Is this fair?	Some students may have had experiences with flipping two coins. If the students recognize the unfairness, suggest that they play the game and test their conclusion.
Divide the class into pairs. Give each pair two pennies: When one student flips, the other records the outcome, and then they exchange roles. Play the game for about two minutes. This gives practice in simulating and collecting data. Discuss. Demonstrate how to tally: Match ~~1111~~ 1 No Match 111 _____ + _____ = _____ Total Matches Total No Matches Total	Let's simulate this game. Recall that playing a game and collecting data (results) to make our decisions is called *simulating*. How should the coins be flipped so that the method of flipping does not affect the outcome?	Various answers.

Activity 2 *Explore*

OBSERVATIONS	POSSIBLE RESPONSES
Check each pair of students to see if they are randomly tossing pennies and tallying correctly.	
Some pairs of students will begin to see the unfairness.	Ask students to start to think of an explanation.

Activity 2 *Summarize*

TEACHER ACTION	TEACHER TALK	EXPECTED RESPONSE
Collect data on the board: Match | No Match _____ + _____ = _____ Total Matches + Total No Matches = Total Experimental Probability (Match) $= \frac{\text{Number of matches}}{\text{Total number of trials}}$	Before we collect the data from the entire class, do you think the game is fair? If we get the totals for the numerator and the denominator of our probabilities by counting frequencies from our experimental results, we refer to these as *experimental* probabilities. Let's calculate the experimental probabilities of getting a match and a no match.	Most pairs will have collected data to support the unfairness of the game. The results should yield probabilities close to $\frac{1}{2}$.
Ask.	Why is the game unfair?	There are as many ways to get a match as a no match. Because Player B gets more points for a no match, the game is unfair.
Collect answers and write HT, HH, TH, TT on the board.	Let's see if we can analyze what happens in the game. What are the possibilities when we flip two coins?	First coin could be H and second coin could be T, etc.
Write on the board. Ask.	Here is another way of listing all the outcomes.	

TEACHER ACTION	TEACHER TALK	EXPECTED RESPONSE
First Penny / Second Penny / Possible Outcomes: H — H: HH H — T: HT T — H: TH T — T: TT	What are the possibilities when we flip the first penny?	H or T.
	If heads (H) comes up what can happen for the second penny?	Still H or T.
	If tails (T) comes up on the first coin, what can happen on the second?	H or T.
	We call this diagram a *tree* diagram because it looks like the branches of a tree.	
	What are all the possible outcomes?	HH, HT, TH, TT.
	How many are matches? How many are no matches?	Two matches: HH, TT. Two no matches: HT, TH.
	How can we make this a fair game?	Change the points so that each player gets the same number.
Review the definition of probability by asking questions about the outcomes of flipping two coins.	If we determine the numerators and denominators for our probabilities by using the list we made of all possible outcomes, we call these *theoretical* probabilities.	
Write out the probability statement each time.	What is the probability of getting 2 heads?	$P(HH) = \frac{1}{4}$
	What is the probability of getting 2 tails?	$P(TT) = \frac{1}{4}$
	What is the probability of getting a head and a tail?	$P(HT \text{ or } TH) = \frac{2}{4} \text{ or } \frac{1}{2}$
	What is the probability of getting a match? No match?	$P(Match) = \frac{2}{4} \text{ or } \frac{1}{2}$; $P(No\ Match) = \frac{2}{4} \text{ or } \frac{1}{2}$
	How do these results compare to our class *experimental* results?	Good. If not good discuss what may have caused the discrepancy. Stress that theoretical probabilities indicate what should happen over a long time. The more trials, the more likely we are to approach the theoretical data.

TEACHER ACTION	TEACHER TALK	EXPECTED RESPONSE
Ask.	What is the probability of getting at *least* one head?	$\frac{3}{4}$ (HH, HT, TH)
	What is the probability of getting at *most* one head?	$\frac{3}{4}$ (TT, TH, HT) Students tend to overlook TT as satisfying this question; if so, discuss the meaning of *at most.*
Pose game 1 and 2. Pass out chips. Pass out Worksheet 2-1.	Game 1: Two chips: one chip with the letter x on both sides. One chip with an x on one side and a y on the other side. Rules: Flip both chips. Score: Player I gets a point if there is a match. Player II gets a point if there is no match.	
Ask. Make sure the class votes on the fairness first.	Is this a fair game? Why?	Most students will say no; x can occur more often.
Record the votes on the board.	Game 2: Three chips: one chip with an A on one side and a B on the other side; one chip with an A on one side and a C on the other side; one chip with a B on one side and a C on the other side. Rules: Flip all three chips at the same time. Score: Player I gets a point if any two chips match. Player II gets a point if all three chips are different.	
	Is this a fair game? Why?	Various answers; fair because same number of letters; unfair because it is easier to match.

Activity 2 *Summarize*

TEACHER ACTION	TEACHER TALK	EXPECTED RESPONSE
Let the student pairs play the games; students should take turns flipping and recording.		
Allow 5–10 minutes for students to play both games.		
Make sure each pair calculates an experimental probability based on their trials. You might suggest the trials for game 1 be in multiples of 10 and the trials for game 2 be in multiples of 8. This will make it easier to compare the experimental and theoretical probabilities.		

Activity 2 *Explore*

OBSERVATIONS	POSSIBLE RESPONSES
	As you move around the room observe the surprise of some students as they discover that the first chip has no influence on the outcome.
Some students may have difficulty flipping chips.	Shaking chips in a paper cup is helpful.
Students will begin to see the unfairness of game 2.	Ask students to think of how they might make game 2 fair. Ask what outcomes were possible. Were there more matches with A than B or C, etc?

TEACHER ACTION	TEACHER TALK	EXPECTED RESPONSE
Discuss game 1. Record some of the probabilities obtained from the class.	Is this a fair game? Why?	Yes; each player has the same chance of winning.
Ask.	Were you surprised?	Yes; the first chip has no effect on the outcome.
	What are all the possible outcomes?	xx, xy
List outcomes on the board as students give them.	How many ways to get each?	Two: xx, xx; xy, xy.
Analyze game 1 by putting a tree diagram on the board.	Perhaps we can see this better if we use a tree.	
Ask.	What are the possible outcomes?	Four: xx, xy, xx, xy.
	What is the probability of a match?	$\frac{2}{4}$ or $\frac{1}{2}$
	What is the probability of a no match?	$\frac{2}{4}$ or $\frac{1}{2}$
	How do these results compare with the results in each group?	They are quite close.
	Why is there a difference?	Difficult to flip chips randomly; chips stick together; did not do enough trials, etc.
Discuss.	When we simulate a situation we assume we are generating our data *randomly*. Random means that the outcomes occur by chance.	
Discuss game 2. Collect and record some of the class probabilities; or determine the probability based on the data from entire class.		
Ask.	Is this a fair game?	No. Player I wins more often than Player II.
	Would you rather rely on your data or use the entire class data?	Class data; small samples may not be large enough to decide.

Tree diagram:

1st Chip	2nd Chip	All Outcomes
x	x	xx
	y	xy
x	x	xx
	y	xy

TEACHER ACTION	TEACHER TALK	EXPECTED RESPONSE
Have students *list* outcomes first.	What are some ways the chips could land?	AAC, BCB, ACC, etc.
Analyze game 2 by putting a tree diagram on the board.	Let's see why this appears to be unfair, using a tree diagram to find all the outcomes.	Students may need help reading this three branch tree.

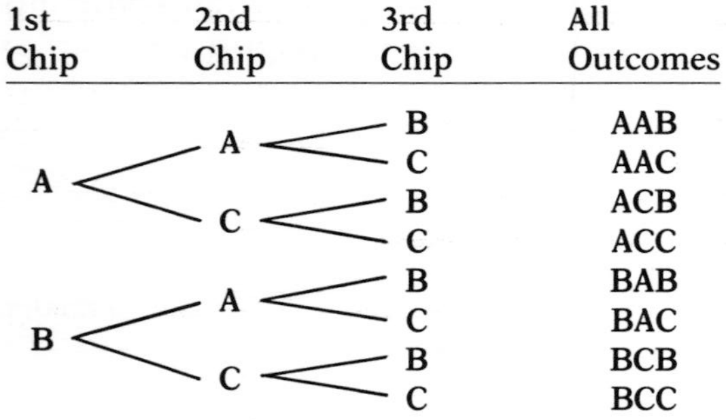

1st Chip	2nd Chip	3rd Chip	All Outcomes
A	A	B	AAB
		C	AAC
	C	B	ACB
		C	ACC
B	A	B	BAB
		C	BAC
	C	B	BCB
		C	BCC

TEACHER ACTION	TEACHER TALK	EXPECTED RESPONSE
Ask.	How many of the eight outcomes are a match?	Six: AAB, AAC, ACC, BAB, BCB, BCC.
	What is the probability of Player I winning?	$\frac{6}{8}$ or $\frac{3}{4}$
	What is the probability of Player II winning?	$\frac{2}{8}$ or $\frac{1}{4}$
	How do these probabilities compare with the class trials (experiments)?	They are quite close.
Be sure to discuss the probabilities in each of the suggested rule changes.	How can we make this a fair game?	Change the points: Player I gets 1 point for a match and Player II gets 3 points for a no match.
	Is there any other way we can make this a fair game?	Change the rules: Player I wins on a pair of As, Player II wins on a pair of Bs. Everything else is a tie.
Pass out Worksheet 2-2, More Chips. Problem 3 has the students make up a fair, two person game. You may wish to hand out these games as another assignment, having the class decide the fairness of each, or, discuss some of the games in class.		Or, Player I wins on a pair of As and a pair of Cs. Player II wins on a pair of Bs and no matches.

NAME ______________________

Chips

Game 1

Materials: Two chips—one with the letter x on both sides and one with an x on one side and a y on the other side.

Rules: Flip both chips at once.

Score: Player I gets a point if the chips match.
Player II gets a point if the chips do not match.

Play and Record:

	Player I Match	Player II No Match
Tally		
Total	______ +	______ = ______

P(Match) = ______

P(No Match) = ______

Game 2

Materials: Three chips—1 chip with an A side and a B side
1 chip with an A side and a C side
1 chip with a B side and a C side

Rules: Flip all three chips at once.

Score: Player I gets a point if there is a match.
Player II gets a point if there is no match.

Play and Record:

	Player I Match	Player II No Match
Tally		
Total	______ +	______ = ______

P(Match) = ______

P(No Match) = ______

NAME ____________________

More Chips

Decide whether the following games are fair or unfair by analyzing each game with a tree diagram.

1. Players have two red chips each with an A side and a B side, and one blue chip with an A side and a B side. Flip all three chips. Player I wins if both red chips show A, if the blue chip shows A, or if all chips show A. Otherwise Player II wins.

2. Players have three yellow chips, each with an A side and a B side, and one green chip with an A side and a B side. Flip all four chips. Player I wins if all three yellow chips show A, if the green chip shows A, or if all chips show A. Otherwise Player II wins.

3. Invent a fair game for two people using three coins. Write down the rules and how the game is to be scored.

Activity 3

FAIR AND UNFAIR GAMES II

OVERVIEW

The theme of analyzing fair and unfair games is continued in this activity, however, the focus is on games played with two dice. These games yield more possible outcomes to consider. The first game is based on the sum of the two numbers that result when the dice are tossed. The second game is based on the product of the two numbers. In both games, one player scores if the sum or product is even and the other player scores if the sum or product is odd. Note: At all times we are making the assumption that the dice being tossed are always fair.

Attempting a tree diagram or a list becomes a cumbersome way to find all possible outcomes when dice are tossed. An easier way to analyze the problem is to use a chart or table. Each game has 36 outcomes. The sum game is fair: There are 18 even sums and 18 odd sums. The different sums range from 2 to 12 with the sum of 7 being most frequent. The product game is unfair: There are 27 even products and 9 odd products. The different products range from 1 to 36.

The students have further practice in determining and comparing experimental and theoretical probabilities. In addition, they are asked to reassign points so that a situation such as P(odd product) = $\frac{1}{4}$ and P(even product) = $\frac{3}{4}$ can be made fair for both players. Most students recognize that 3 points for A and 1 point for B on each score will produce a fair game. With a game in which P(product is a multiple of 4) = $\frac{15}{36}$ and P(product is a multiple of 3) = $\frac{20}{36}$ the students take a bit longer to see that 20 points for A and 15 points for B on each score will make the game fair. (Some students will recognize that 4 points for A and 3 points for B will also work. If your students have studied the least common multiple of two numbers, then you can use this strategy to find the least common multiple of 15 and 20; it is 60, so students need to multiply 15 by 4 and 20 by 3 to make the game fair.)

Goals for students

1. Practice performing a simulation.
2. Determine experimental probabilities.
3. Determine theoretical probabilities.
4. Compare experimental and theoretical probabilities.
5. Organize and analyze data by using a chart or table.
6. Decide whether a game or situation is fair.
7. Make an unfair game fair by assigning points or by changing the rules.

Materials

30 dice.

15 dice of a different color (Optional).

Worksheets

3-1, Two Dice Games.

*3-2, Analyzing Two-Dice Games.

3-3, More Dice Games.

Transparencies

Starred item should be made into a transparency.

FAIR AND UNFAIR GAMES II

TEACHER ACTION	TEACHER TALK	EXPECTED RESPONSE
Tell. You may wish to start by analyzing some of the three penny games invented by students (Worksheet 2-2).	Today we will analyze some games that involve dice.	
Hold up one die. Explain and ask.	This is a die, which I will roll. If an even number comes up, I win a point. If an odd number comes up, you win a point.	
	Is this fair? Why?	Yes; there are six numbers—three are even (2, 4, 6), three are odd (1, 3, 5).
	What is the P(even)?	$\frac{1}{2}$
	What is the P(odd)?	$\frac{1}{2}$
Explain. Don't yet tell the students that the game is fair (there are the same number of even outcomes as odd outcomes).	I would like you to analyze two games, each of which involves two dice. Game 1 *Materials:* 2 dice. *Rules:* Roll both dice. Add the two numbers. *Score:* Player A gets a point if the sum on the dice is even. Player B gets a point if the sum on the dice is odd.	
Ask. Have the students vote. At this stage you simply want to focus on their reasoning without spoiling the surprise of the experiment.	Is this game fair or unfair? Why?	Various answers; if students claim the game is unfair, ask whom the game favors.

TEACHER ACTION	TEACHER TALK	EXPECTED RESPONSE
As a mini-challenge, get the class started on recording the results of throwing the two dice.	Investigate this game by tossing two dice, finding the sum, and recording the results.	
Ask.	What are the numbers we might get as sums?	2, 3, 4, 5, 6, 7, 8, 9, 10, 11, 12
	Let's record the results of the tosses of two dice on a grid:	
Illustrate.		

					x						
	x		x	x	x		x				
Sum	2	3	4	5	6	7	8	9	10	11	12
Total number of times sum occurred.											

TEACHER ACTION	TEACHER TALK	EXPECTED RESPONSE
Toss a pair of dice a few times and put an X in the appropriate column. For example, if you toss sums of 2, 4, 5, 6, 6, and 8, the grid will look like the illustration.	To investigate the game, toss the dice several times and record the results on the grid on your worksheet. Be careful to space your Xs so that they are the same size; put the same space between each X in a column.	
Pass out Worksheet 3-1.		
Explain.	Let's look at the second game.	
	Game 2 is the same as game 1 except you multiply the two numbers instead of adding them. Record the products on page 2 of the worksheet.	
Ask.	Is this fair? Why?	Various answers.
Have students vote.		

Activity 3 *Launch*

TEACHER ACTION	TEACHER TALK	EXPECTED RESPONSE
Play a couple of turns with the class.		Play the game and collect tallies of entire class.
Ask.	How can we decide?	
Review.	Playing the game and collecting data to mold our decisions is called *simulating*.	
Ask.	What numbers are possible products when we toss two dice?	1, 2, 3, 4, 5, 6, 8, 9, 10, 12, 15, 16, 18, 20, 24, 25, 30, 36.
Divide the class into pairs. Give each pair of students a set of dice.		
Allow 5–10 minutes for students to play both games. Have students take turns rolling the dice and recording the results.	Continue to play both games. Record the results on the grids on your worksheet.	

Activity 3 *Explore*

OBSERVATIONS	POSSIBLE RESPONSES
	Check simulating and tallying procedures in each group.
Some students may think that there is only one way to get a sum of 3.	Use different colored dice to stress that 1 + 2 is different from 2 + 1.

TEACHER ACTION	TEACHER TALK	EXPECTED RESPONSE
Discuss game 1 first.		
Ask.	Is game 1 a fair game?	Most students will say yes.
	What is the probability of getting an even sum? What is the probability of getting an odd sum?	Various answers; discuss possible causes for discrepancies.
	How can we decide?	Use the entire class data.
Collect and record from the various groups the total outcomes. Sums: Even | Odd ______ + ______ = ______ Total Evens + Total Odds = Total Outcomes	Based on the class results, calculate the probabilities. What are they?	The entire class results should yield answers that are very close to $\frac{1}{2}$.
Hold up a good histogram to illustrate.	The grids on which you recorded your tosses give you a visual picture of the results. If you were careful to make the spacing of your Xs uniform, you have a special graph of the results, called a histogram. From a histogram, we can tell at a glance which sums occurred most often.	
Discuss the value of a large number of trials vs. a small number of trials.		
Try to get students to appreciate that over a long period of many trials the average tends to stabilize to the theoretical probabilities.		

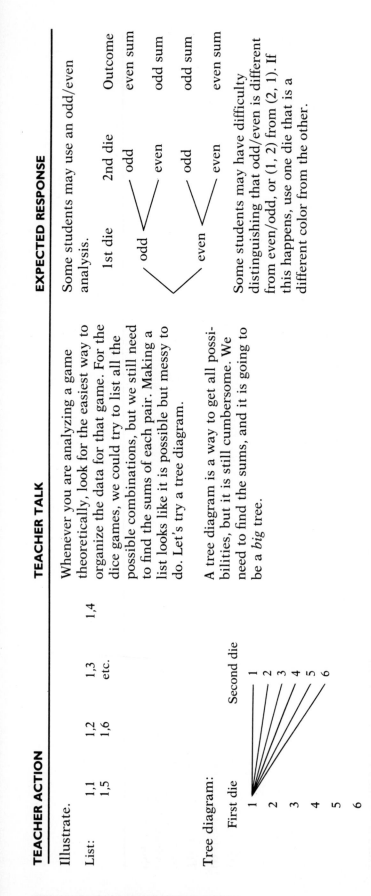

TEACHER ACTION	TEACHER TALK	EXPECTED RESPONSE
Illustrate. List: 1,1 1,2 1,3 1,4 1,5 1,6 etc.	Whenever you are analyzing a game theoretically, look for the easiest way to organize the data for that game. For the dice games, we could try to list all the possible combinations, but we still need to find the sums of each pair. Making a list looks like it is possible but messy to do. Let's try a tree diagram.	Some students may use an odd/even analysis. 1st die — 2nd die — Outcome odd — odd — even sum odd — even — odd sum even — odd — odd sum even — even — even sum
Tree diagram: First die — Second die 1 — 1, 2, 3, 4, 5, 6 2 3 4 5 6	A tree diagram is a way to get all possibilities, but it is still cumbersome. We need to find the sums, and it is going to be a *big* tree.	Some students may have difficulty distinguishing that odd/even is different from even/odd, or (1, 2) from (2, 1). If this happens, use one die that is a different color from the other.

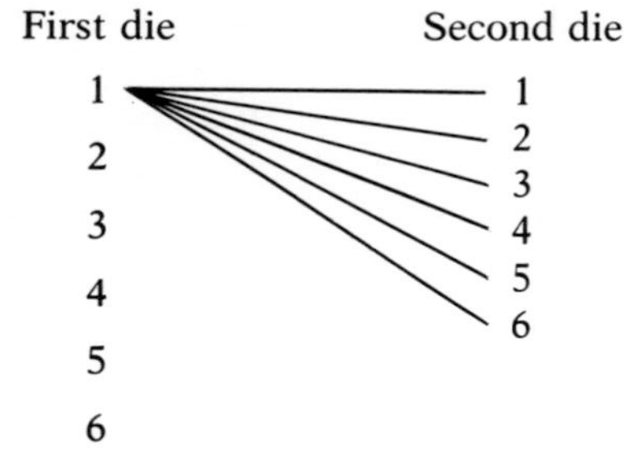

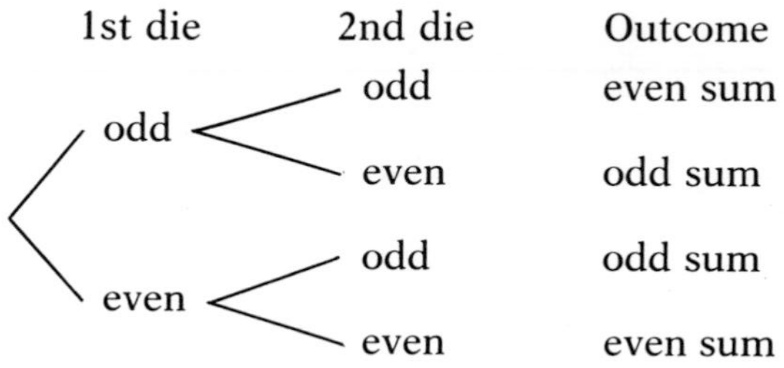

TEACHER ACTION | **TEACHER TALK** | **EXPECTED RESPONSE**

Teacher Action: Pass out Worksheet 3-2, Analyzing Two-Dice Game. Put transparency of Worksheet 3-2 on the overhead projector.

Teacher Talk: Another way to organize and analyze our data is by making a chart. A chart turns out to be very convenient in this situation.

Teacher Action:

Game 1

Sum

	1	2	3	4	5	6
1						
2						
3						
4						
5						
6						

Teacher Talk: The numbers on the left of the chart represent the first die and the numbers across the top represent the second die.

To fill in a spot in the chart, look to see how the first die landed and how the second die landed. Then add and record the sum.

Teacher Action: Illustrate first row.

	1	2	3	4	5	6
1	2	3	4	5	6	7
2						
3						
4						
5						
6						

Teacher Talk: Let's do the first row together. The pair 1,1 gives us a sum of 2. The pair 1,2 gives us a sum of 3 and so on.

Teacher Action: Complete chart.

Teacher Talk: Now you complete your chart as I fill in this one.

Expected Response:

Game 1

Sum

	1	2	3	4	5	6
1	2	3	4	5	6	7
2	3	4	5	6	7	8
3	4	5	6	7	8	9
4	5	6	7	8	9	10
5	6	7	8	9	10	11
6	7	8	9	10	11	12

Activity 3 *Summarize*

TEACHER ACTION	TEACHER TALK	EXPECTED RESPONSE
With the filled out chart on the overhead, ask.	What numbers occurred as sums?	2, 3, 4, 5, 6, 7, 8, 9, 10, 11, 12.
	Which sum occurred most frequently?	7
	What is the total number of ways the two dice can land?	36
	How many pairs have an odd sum?	18
	How many pairs have an even sum?	18
	What is the P(odd sum)?	$\frac{18}{36} = \frac{1}{2}$
	What is the P(even sum)?	$\frac{18}{36} = \frac{1}{2}$
	What did we find from our class experiment about P(odd sum) and P(even sum)?	The experimental result was very close to the theoretical result.
	What is the probability of getting each sum?	$P(2) = \frac{1}{36}$ $P(7) = \frac{6}{36}$ $P(3) = \frac{2}{36}$ $P(8) = \frac{5}{36}$ $P(4) = \frac{3}{36}$ $P(9) = \frac{4}{36}$ $P(5) = \frac{4}{36}$ $P(10) = \frac{3}{36}$ $P(6) = \frac{5}{36}$ $P(11) = \frac{2}{36}$ $P(12) = \frac{1}{36}$

TEACHER ACTION	TEACHER TALK	EXPECTED RESPONSE
Students may enjoy looking at other patterns in the chart. There are many other probability questions that could be explored. Have students pose a probability question and use the chart to solve it.	What is the probability that the sum is less than 7?	$\frac{15}{36}$
	What is the probability that the sum is greater than 7?	$\frac{15}{36}$
	What is the probability that the sum is a multiple of 3?	$\frac{12}{36}$
	What is the probability that the sum is a multiple of 4?	$\frac{9}{36}$
Discuss game 2.		
Ask.	Is this a fair game?	No.
Collect and record the total class results.	Whom does it favor?	The player with the even products.
Product Even | Odd _____ + _____ = _____ Total Evens + Total Odds = Total Outcomes		
Ask.	Based on the class results, what are the probabilities?	P(E) will be close to $\frac{3}{4}$. P(O) will be close to $\frac{1}{4}$.
Complete the product chart on the transparency of Worksheet 3-2 with the class.	Let's analyze this game with a chart.	Game 2 Product

Game 2 — Product

	1	2	3	4	5	6
1	1	2	3	4	5	6
2	2	4	6	8	10	12
3	3	6	9	12	15	18
4	4	8	12	16	20	24
5	5	10	15	20	25	30
6	6	12	18	24	30	36

TEACHER ACTION	TEACHER TALK	EXPECTED RESPONSE
Ask.	What are the total number of products?	36
	What is the P(even product)?	$\frac{27}{36} = \frac{3}{4}$
	What is the P(odd product)?	$\frac{9}{36} = \frac{1}{4}$
	These are theoretical probabilities. We wrote experimental probabilities based on our class data.	
	How did the two sets of probabilities compare?	They are very close.
	If the experimental results do not match the theoretical results, does it mean our experiment was bad?	No; it was an experiment and we may have just gotten an unlikely, but possible, distribution.
Ask.	How can we make the product game a fair game without changing the rules?	Change the points. Give B 3 points for each odd.
	How could we change the rules and make this a fair game?	Collect and analyze some suggestions from the class; for example, one person scores a point for any product from 2–10, and the other person scores a point if products equal 1 or any number 12–36.
Repeat some of the questions from the summary of game 3. Encourage students to make up other probability questions using the data in the chart.		
Pass out Worksheet 3-3, More Dice Games.		

NAME ______________________

Two-Dice Games

Game I

Materials: Two dice

Rules: Roll both dice. Add the two numbers.

Score: Player I scores a point if the sum is even.
Player II scores a point if the sum is odd.

Play and record the actual sum in the appropriate column.

Sum	2	3	4	5	6	7	8	9	10	11	12
Total number of times sum occurred											

Based on your results:

Number of even sums rolled = ________

Number of odd sums rolled = ________

Total number of trials = ________

P (odd sum) = ________

P (even sum) = ________

NAME

Two-Dice Games

Game 2

Materials: Two dice

Rules: Roll both dice. Multiply the two numbers.

Score: Player I scores a point if the product is even.
Player II scores a point if the product is odd.

Play and record the actual product in the appropriate column.

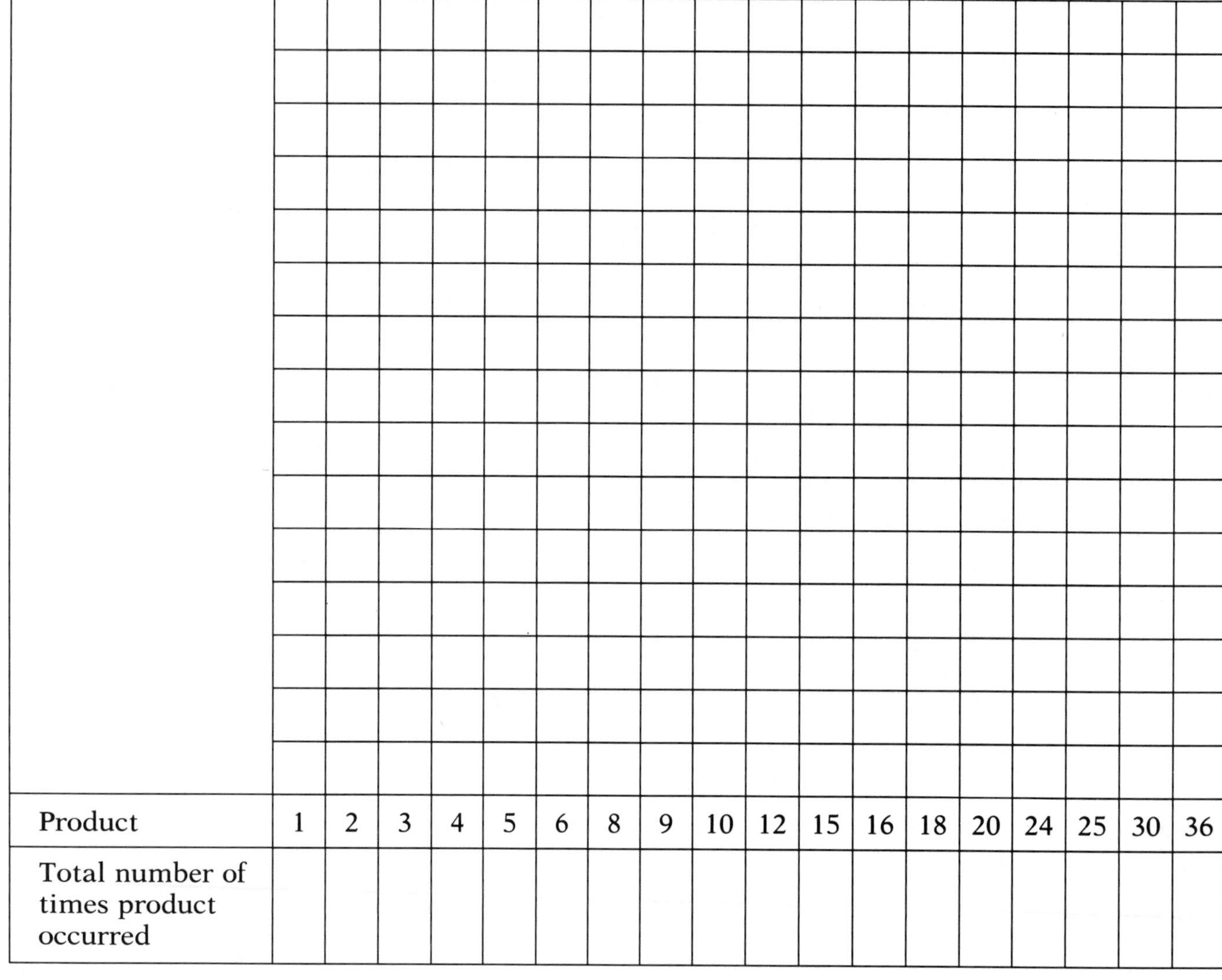

Product	1	2	3	4	5	6	8	9	10	12	15	16	18	20	24	25	30	36
Total number of times product occurred																		

Based on your results:

Number of even products rolled = ______

Number of odd products rolled = ______

Total number of trials = ______

P (odd product) = ______

P (even product) = ______

NAME ____________________

Analyzing Two-Dice Games

Game 1
Sum

	1	2	3	4	5	6
1						
2						
3						
4						
5						
6						

Total sums = ________

Total number of even sums = ________

Total number of odd sums = ________

P (even sum) = ________

P (odd sum) = ________

Game 2
Product

	1	2	3	4	5	6
1						
2						
3						
4						
5						
6						

Total products = ________

Total number of even products = ________

Total number of odd products = ________

P (even product) = ________

P (odd product) = ________

NAME ______________________

More Dice Games

1. A pair of dice are tossed. Find the probability of getting

   A sum of 3 ________

   A sum of 9 ________

   A sum greater than 7 ________

   A sum which is a multiple of 3 ________

   A sum which is a multiple of 4 ________

   A product of 12 ________

   A product greater than 12 ________

   A product less than 12 ________

   A product that is a multiple of 5 ________

   A product that is a multiple of 3 or 4 ________

Decide whether games 3 and 4 are fair or unfair. If unfair, who has the advantage? Describe a way to assign points to make it fair.

Game 3

Toss two dice. Subtract the smaller number from the larger number. Player I scores one point if the difference is odd. Player II scores one point if the difference is even. (Note: Zero is an even number.)

	1	2	3	4	5	6
1						
2						
3						
4						
5						
6						

Game 4

Toss two dice. Find the product.
Player I scores one point if the product is a multiple of 4.
Player II scores one point if the product is a multiple of 3.

Computer Activity I HISTOGRAMS

OVERVIEW

This activity uses the computer to simulate tossing two dice 100 or 1,000 times. From this data, the students learn to make histograms. In order to compare theoretical and experimental probabilities in histogram form, the students must convert fractions to decimals (or percents).

Using a computer allows each student to gather data for 100 tosses quickly and allows a group of students to gather data on 1,000 tosses quickly. The variations in how closely the experimental data fits the theoretical distribution in the 100 tosses compared with the 1,000 tosses help students to see the significance of the law of large numbers, i.e., experimental results approach the theoretical distribution as the number of trials increases.

To be most meaningful, this computer activity needs to be taught as a hands-on, interactive experience. Groups of two or three students working together at a machine are ideal. More than two or three at a machine decreases the effectiveness of the activity. If you have only a few machines, rotate groups of students through the activities while others are involved with some other assignment.

Goals for students

1. Learn how to compare two sets of data by using histograms (bar graphs).
2. Observe how experimental results approach theoretical distribution as the number of trials increases (the law of large numbers).
3. Observe variation in results of repeated experiments.
4. Use a computer to generate data.
5. Make a game fair based on known probabilities.

Materials

Microcomputer(s).

Programs—DICE TOSS (Materials CIII-1).
DICE GAME (Materials CIII-2).

(If possible, the pre-recorded programs provided with the unit should be used. Otherwise, the appended programs will provide the necessary information.)

Worksheets

*CI-1, Bar graph.
CI-2, Two Dice.
CI-3, Fair Games.

Transparencies

Starred item should be made into a transparency.

HISTOGRAMS

TEACHER ACTION	TEACHER TALK	EXPECTED RESPONSE
Load a computer with DICE TOSS program. Have students take out their table of sums from Worksheet 3-2. Dice Toss can be found at the end of Computer Activity III (Materials CIII-1).	Let's review the number of ways two dice can fall. We found these in Activity 3 when we made a table of sums.	
Ask.	How many ways can the sum be 3?	2
	How many ways can the sum be 4? etc.?	3
Show Worksheet CI-1 on the overhead projector. Record the totals as given.	How many ways can the two dice fall in all?	36

Possible sums	2	3	4	5	6	7	8	9	10	11	12
Number of Occurrences	1	2	3	4	5	6	5	4	3	2	1
Decimal Equivalents											

TEACHER ACTION	TEACHER TALK	EXPECTED RESPONSE
Simulate 100 tosses on the computer and use the generated results. (The numbers given below are just an example.)	I have put a program in the computer that will simulate tossing two dice and adding the numbers tossed. We can toss as many times as we want. Let's toss 100 times.	
	Are these results what we'd expect? Look at the 7s. We got 19 out of 100.	Various answers. Have students discuss their ideas.
	How do we compare 6 out of 36 with 19 out of 100?	The two are quite close; have students use decimals to figure exactly.
The computer program will display decimal equivalents if you remove the REM in line 100. If you want the students to make these conversions themselves, have a few calculators available.	$\frac{6}{36} = .17$ $\frac{19}{100} = .19$	
	What does this say? Did we get as many 7s as we'd expected?	We got a few more.

2	3	4	5	6	7	8	9	10	11	12
1	2	11	10	19	19	13	5	12	7	1

TEACHER ACTION	TEACHER TALK	EXPECTED RESPONSE
Show students that the key sequence $6 \div 36 =$ gives the decimal equivalent for $\frac{6}{36}$.		
	Let's convert the theoretical and experimental results to decimal equivalents.	
Ask.	What's $\frac{1}{36}$?	.0277777 . . .
	Let's round this to .03	
100 Tosses—Theoretical	$\frac{2}{36} = .05555\ldots \approx .06$, etc.	

Possible sums	2	3	4	5	6	7	8	9	10	11	12
Number of Occurrences	1	2	3	4	5	6	5	4	3	2	1
Decimal Equivalents	.03	.06	.08	.11	.14	.17	.14	.11	.08	.06	.03

TEACHER ACTION	TEACHER TALK	EXPECTED RESPONSE
Ask.	The experimental data is easy. We have $\frac{1}{100}, \frac{2}{100}, \frac{11}{100}$, etc. What are these converted to decimals?	.01, etc.
100 Tosses—Experimental		

Possible sums	2	3	4	5	6	7	8	9	10	11	12
Number of Occurrences	1	2	11	10	19	19	13	5	12	7	1
Decimal Equivalents	.01	.02	.11	.10	.19	.19	.13	.05	.12	.07	.01

Computer Activity I
Launch

TEACHER ACTION	TEACHER TALK	EXPECTED RESPONSE
Explain.	It is sometimes difficult to tell how close two sets of data are by simply looking at numbers. Making a graph or picture of the data allows us to immediately see how close the two are.	
	Let's make a bar graph of both the theoretical and experimental results for two dice.	
Pass out Worksheet CI-1, Bar Graph. Direct students through the page using the overhead projector.	First copy the theoretical and experimental results on your worksheet in the space provided.	
Illustrate how to find the tops of the bars. Mark them in one color. Continue at the overhead until the students have done the entire bar graph correctly.	Now on the grid mark the data for the theoretical results. The probability that a sum of 2 can occur is .03, so we draw the top of a bar at .03 directly over the number 2 on the base line.	
Mark experimental values with colored pen.	Now mark the experimental values, using a different color. Over 2, mark .01 (or whatever the computer result was).	
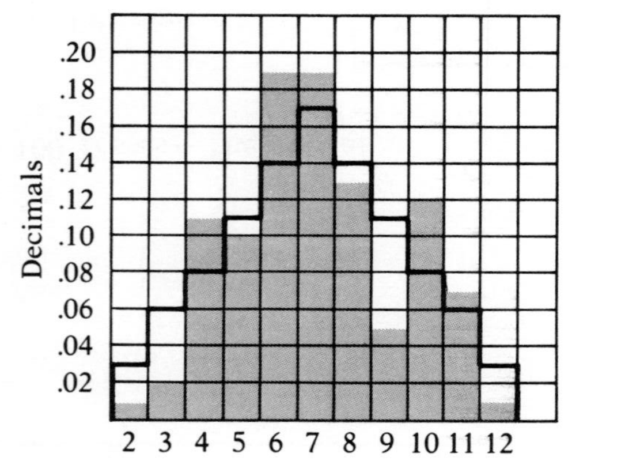 *(This illustrates the histogram done with decimals.)*	How are the graphs the same?	Various answers.
	How are they different?	Both are small at ends and large in the middle; experiment is not symmetric.

TEACHER ACTION	TEACHER TALK	EXPECTED RESPONSE
Ask.	If we tossed a pair of dice 100 times, could we get a distribution as different from the theoretical as the computer did?	Yes.
	If we each tossed a pair of dice 100 times would all our distributions be alike?	No.
	How could we improve our chances of getting a distribution closer to the theoretical distribution?	Increase the number of tosses.
Pass out Worksheet CI-2, Two Dice.	We are going to use the computer to generate a distribution for 100 and 1,000 tosses. A larger number of tosses should give us distributions closer to the theoretical result. Each of you in a group should get your own data for 100 tosses. Then each group at a computer should run the experiment for 1,000 tosses only once. (This takes time.) The entire group should use the same data for 1,000. Copy the results for each set of data. Express the frequency of each outcome as a decimal equivalent and then draw the histogram to show your results. The histogram for the theoretical results is already drawn on your grid. Draw your histogram on top using a colored pencil.	

OBSERVATIONS	POSSIBLE RESPONSES
	When students in a group have collected their data for 100, encourage them to do their histogram while the computer does the 1,000 run. Go from group to group focusing students' attention with comments such as "You got a lot of 8s. Were you short on any result?" "Is your histogram going to look like the one we did together? How will it differ?"

Computer Activity I
Summarize

TEACHER ACTION	TEACHER TALK	EXPECTED RESPONSE
Run 100 tosses on the computer to use as experimental data.	Let's look at some games to determine if they are fair or unfair.	
	Game 1: If you roll a 6, you gain 5 points. Otherwise, you lose 1 point.	
	How many times would we have won if we used the experimental results we just ran on the computer?	Gain □ times Lose □ times (numbers are an example.)
	How many points did we gain?	□ × 5 = □ points
	What's our loss?	□ × 1 = □ points
	What is the difference or net gain?	□ − □ = □ points
	Is this a fair game?	Various answers; try to elicit that in a win-lose scoring situation, a fair game is one that gives a zero net gain.
	If we tossed 36 times in a theoretical world, we'd gain on 5 and lose on 31 of them. We'd gain 5 points 5 times. We'd lose 1 point 31 times.	
	So we'd gain 5 × 5 = 25 points and lose 31 points for a net loss of 6 points.	
	So this is an unfair game.	
	Game 2: If the sum of the roll is even, you gain 1 point; if the sum of the roll is odd, you lose 1 point.	
	How many times would we have gained? Use the experimental results.	Gain □ Lose □
	What's our net gain (gains minus losses)?	□ − □ = □
	We played the even-odd game in Activity 3. Was it a fair game?	Yes.
	Is this a fair game?	No.

Computer Activity I
Summarize

TEACHER ACTION	TEACHER TALK	EXPECTED RESPONSE
	Game 3: You gain points if the total shown on the dice is divisible by three. You lose 1 point if it's not divisible by 3. How many points should you get each time you gain to make the game fair?	2 points.
	Why?	P(total is divisible by 3) = $\frac{12}{36}$ 2 ways to get 3 5 ways to get 6 4 ways to get 9 1 way to get 12 12 ways
	P(gain) = $\frac{1}{3}$, P(loss) = $\frac{2}{3}$.	
	If you tossed 3 times in a theoretical world, you'd gain on 1 and lose on 2 of the tosses. You'd gain 2 points one time. You'd lose 1 point two times.	
	In 100 throws what happens?	
	Find the number of gains.	27 gains
	Find the number of losses and the net gain.	73 losses $(27 \times 2) - (73 \times 1) = -19$
	A negative net gain is what?	A loss.
	Looking at our data for 100 tosses shows that the experimental results can differ from the theoretical results enough to make basing decisions on the experiment alone risky.	

TEACHER ACTION	TEACHER TALK	EXPECTED RESPONSE
Pass out Worksheet CI-3, Fair Games. Give students time to complete it.	Now it's your turn to analyze some games. Use your experimental results from Worksheet CI-2 to predict whether or not the games are fair.	
Present this game for an extra challenge.	You win 2 points if the sum shown on the dice is divisible by 3; otherwise you lose a point.	
	Is this game fair?	Yes.
	Now let's look at Worksheet CI-3 together.	
Make a list as students supply results.	What were your net gains for the game with 100 tosses?	
Game 1 100: +20, −1, ⋮ 1,000: +2, ⋮	What were your net gains for the game with 1,000 tosses?	
You will have more 100s than 1,000s, but the point to be made is that the 100s will vary much more than the 1,000s.	What do you think the net would be like if we played 10,000 games?	Very small.
	Could it be large?	It could, but it's not very likely.
	Is this a fair game?	Yes; $5 \times \frac{1}{6} = 1 \times \frac{5}{6}$, so the difference between them is zero.

Computer Activity I
Summarize

TEACHER ACTION	TEACHER TALK	EXPECTED RESPONSE
Make a similar list on the board or overhead.	Now let's look at game data. Let's analyze game 2 theoretically.	
Ask.	What's the probability the sum is 2 or 12?	$\frac{2}{36}$
	In 36 tosses in a perfect world, how many points would we gain?	$2 \times 15 = 30$
	How many points would we lose?	$34 \times 1 = 34$
	In 36 tosses we'd expect a net loss of 4 points, so the game is unfair.	
	In $3 \times 36 = 108$ tosses how many points would we expect to lose?	$3 \times 4 = 12$
	How close did our runs of 100 come to this expected result?	Some were close; some were off.
	In $28 \times 36 = 1{,}008$ tosses we would expect to lose $28 \times 4 = 112$ points.	
	How do these compare with the experimental results?	They are much closer.
	We have analyzed game C earlier. Was it a fair game?	Yes.
	So in 100 tosses we would expect an even number 50 times an odd number 50 times, for a result of 0.	
Make a list on the board as students give results.	Look at your 100 tosses and compare results.	
Repeat for 1,000.		
The results for 1,000 are usually very close to the theoretical results.		

NAME ______________________

Bar Graph

Two Dice

100 Tosses—Theoretical

Possible sums	2	3	4	5	6	7	8	9	10	11	12
Number of Occurrences											
Decimal Equivalents											

100 Tosses—Experimental

Possible sums	2	3	4	5	6	7	8	9	10	11	12
Number of Occurrences											
Decimal Equivalents											

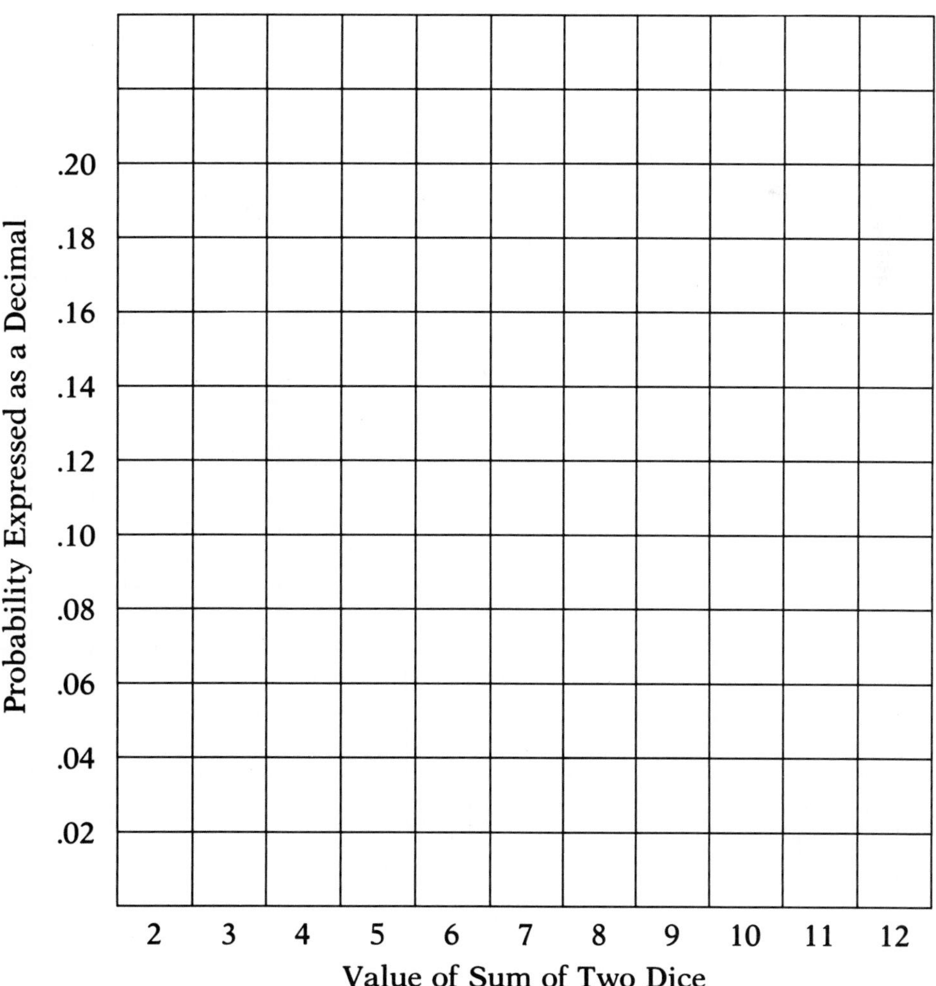

NAME ______________________

Two Dice

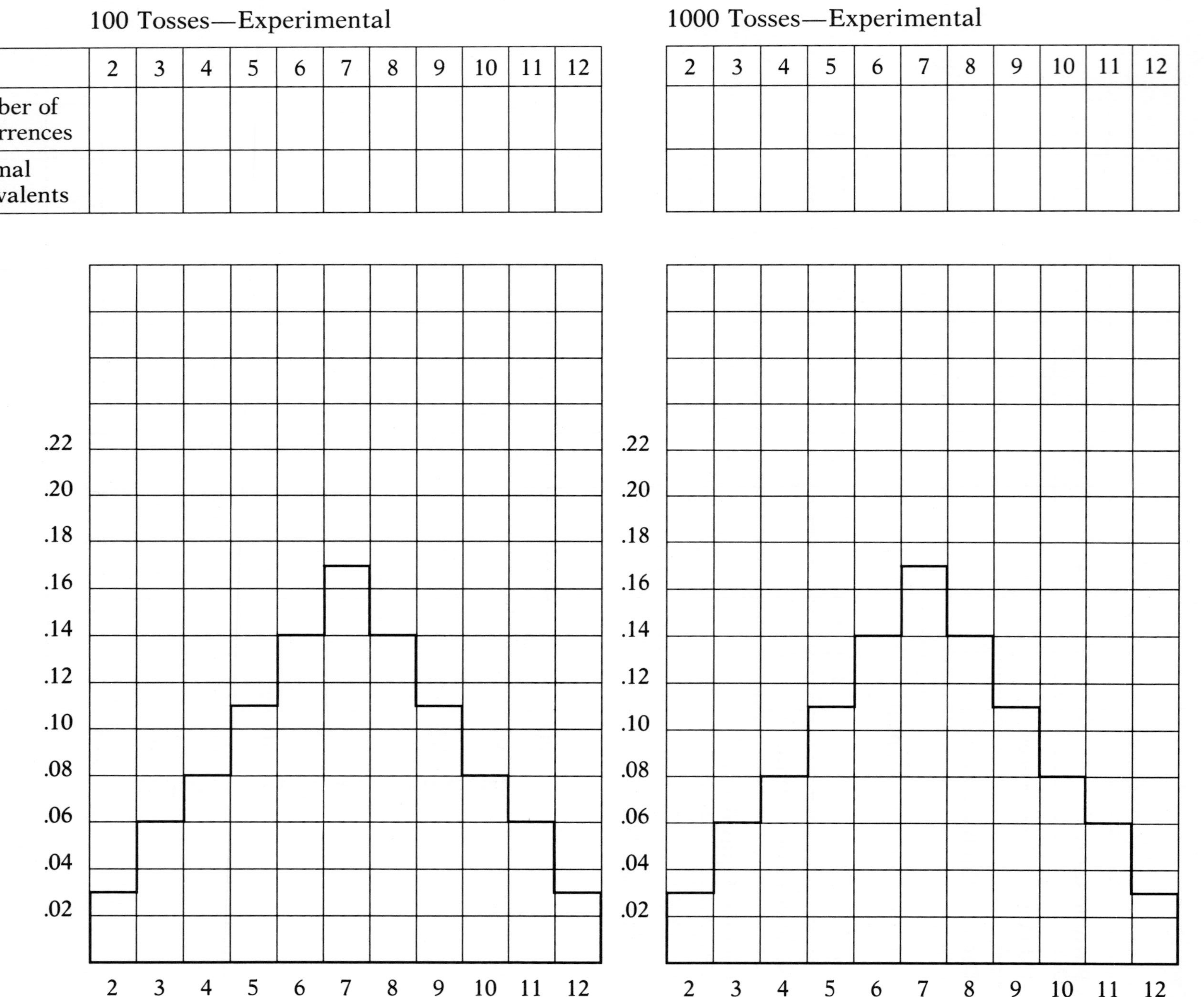

100 Tosses—Experimental

Sum	2	3	4	5	6	7	8	9	10	11	12
Number of Occurrences											
Decimal Equivalents											

1000 Tosses—Experimental

2	3	4	5	6	7	8	9	10	11	12

NAME ______________________

Fair Games?

Use your experimental results from Worksheet CI-2 to answer these questions.

Game A

You gain 5 points if the sum shown on the dice is 7. Otherwise lose 1 point.

Number of 7s	Others

Points Gained	Points Lost

Net Gains

100 Tosses ______

1,000 Tosses ______

Game B

You gain 15 points if the sum shown on the dice is 1 or 12. Otherwise lose 1 point.

Number of 2s or 12s	Others

Points Gained	Points Lost

100 Tosses ______

1,000 Tosses ______

Game C

You gain 1 point if the sum shown on the dice is even. You lose 1 point if the sum is odd.

Number of Even sums	Number of Odd sums

Points Gained	Points Lost

100 Tosses ______

1,000 Tosses ______

Computer Activity II

FAIR GAMES

OVERVIEW

This activity extends the computer work started in Computer Activity I by simulating the playing of a computer-generated game. Students are challenged to make the game fair by selecting an appropriate payoff. The histograms produced in Computer Activity I are the tools the students use to make reasonable beginning estimates of the fair payoff. The computer allows the students quickly to simulate playing the game using a payoff they selected. The results of the simulation help the students to refine their estimates and try again.

Computer Activities I and II together are designed to give students a feeling for the fluctuations one can expect in experimental results. Even more important, the students should begin to see that in making judgments based on experimental data, the nature and number of the trials is extremely important.

Goals for students

1. Attempt to make a game fair, using experimental data.
2. Reinforce observations about variations in results of repeated experiments.
3. See that an increase in the number of trials gives data that more closely approximates the theoretical distributions.

Materials

Microcomputer(s)

Program—DICE GAME (Materials CIII-2).

*Bar Graph (Worksheet CI-1).

Worksheets

*CII-1, Two Dice Game.

Transparencies

Starred items should be made into transparencies.

FAIR GAMES

TEACHER ACTION	TEACHER TALK	EXPECTED RESPONSE
You will need a transparency of Worksheet CII-1, Two Dice Game, and CI-1, Bar Graph. Generate a demonstration game on the computer.	To be the game maker in a two person game, you have to specify on which sum each person will score and how much they will score. In this activity the computer will be the game maker. Each time we run the program, the computer gets to decide on which sums the computer will score points. When the computer gets one of its sums, it always scores 100 points. When one of your sums comes up, you score points, but you have to decide ahead of time how many points you should score so that the game will be a *fair* game. Each group will go to the computer and run the DICE GAME program. When the program asks "How many dice?" enter 2. The program will design a game just for you. On Worksheet CII-1, copy the rules in the place provided.	
Demonstrate the game on Worksheet CII-1. Run the DICE GAME program.	I will demonstrate by having the computer make a game. For this game, the computer scores 100 points if sum is 2, 6, or 8. Otherwise, I score points.	

TEACHER ACTION	TEACHER TALK	EXPECTED RESPONSE
Display Worksheet CI-1 with experimental data. Use data on Worksheet CI-1.	Look at our experimental data for 100 tosses.	
	Had we been playing this game, how many times would the computer have won?	Number of 2s + Number of 6s + Number of 8s = ☐
	How many times would we have won?	Total − Computer = ☐
	How many points would the computer get?	Computer × 100 = ☐
	About how many points should we get each time to make the game fair?	Times we won × points = Computer total
Enter estimated payoff. Run game and copy results on worksheet.	Let's try 50 as a payoff for our score.	
Depending on results, ask.	Is that payoff representative, or was I lucky?	
	How can I tell?	Run again with that payoff.
Direct students to set the payoff and play the game to test their predictions.	Your group will run the program to design a game especially for you.	
	Copy the rules of your game on your worksheet. Use your experimental data on Worksheet CI-2 to help your group plan a good first guess at a payoff for your scores that will make the game fair. For each guess, run the program twice. Experimental results can vary. Based on both runs, revise your guess and try again. Repeat until you think you have a payoff that makes the game fair.	

OBSERVATIONS	POSSIBLE RESPONSES
Students may get a result that looks good on one run of 300. They may want to go with this value without further checks.	Remind students about the fluctuations that resulted in the 100 trials in Computer Activity I. Be sure they do not settle on a value until they have checked each estimate they make at least twice. Ask questions such as "Why did you adjust your estimate down (or up)?" "Why are your two runs with the same payoff different?"
Some students may want to use theoretical data to plan their payoffs. This is actually good thinking on their part and should be encouraged.	

Computer Activity II
Summarize

TEACHER ACTION	TEACHER TALK	EXPECTED RESPONSE
Display a transparency of Worksheet CII-1.	Let's look at the game the computer designed for us when we began.	
Record game rules.	The computer scores if the sum is 2, 6, or 8. Remember our theoretical analysis for two dice.	
	What is the probability that the computer scores?	$\frac{11}{36}$
	What is the probability that we score?	$\frac{25}{36}$
	In a perfect world, if we toss dice 36 times, how many points will the computer get?	$11 \times 100 = 1100$
	How do we determine a fair payoff for us?	$25 \times \text{payoff} - 1100$ $\text{payoff} = \frac{1100}{25}$ $= 44$
Demonstrate in front of class.	Let's use the payoff of 44.	
	To reenter the game in which the computer scores on 2, 6, or 8, we load the DICE GAME program into the computer and type RUN 1290. The program will ask us to type in 2*6*8 to tell the computer when it will score.	
Run game and record results.	Now let's run the game for two sets of 300 tosses with a payoff for our numbers of 44.	

TEACHER ACTION	TEACHER TALK	EXPECTED RESPONSE
Repeat the directions for playing the game if necessary.	On the back of Worksheet CII-1, first write RUN 1290 so you remember how to reenter a game. Then you must type in the numbers on which the computer scores with each number separated by an asterisk (*). Then determine the fair payoff for your game (you may want to use a calculator). Rerun your game, with the fair payoff, for 3 sets of 300 games. Record the results.	
After students finish, let them tell how close to the theoretical value their experimentally fair payoff was.		
For each group, record the rules and their best value. Then as a class compute the theoretically fair payoff and see which group came closest.	Now take one of your games and find the fair payoff by using a theoretical analysis of 36 tosses. Computer scores on ______. Out of 36 tosses, the computer scores on how many tosses? So you score on 36 − ☐ tosses. The computer scores 100 × ☐ points.	Various answers, depending on game specifications.
Continue until each group knows how close their experimentally fair payoff came to the theoretically fair payoff.	You need to score the same number of points to make the game fair. You score (36 − ☐) × payoff points. So 36 − ☐ × payoff = 100 × ☐ or Fair payoff $= \dfrac{100 \times \square}{36 - \square}$	

NAME ______________________

Two-Dice Game

You will need Worksheet CI-2, Two Dice.
Go to the computer and run the program DICE GAME for 2 dice.
The computer will design a game just for you.
Write down the rules on the lines below.

Computer scores 100 points if sum is:	You score if the sum is:
______________________	______________________

Pretend you have been playing this game for 100 tosses.
Look at Worksheet CI-2, Two Dice, to see how many times the computer would score.

Computer scored ______ times.

You scored ______ times.

Computer points = ______.

Find a payoff so that your total points are about the same as the computer's. ______
Enter your first guess and run the program twice.

		Your Score	Computer Score
First Guess / Payoff	First Run	______	______
	Second Run	______	______
Second Guess / Payoff	First Run	______	______
	Second Run	______	______
Third Guess / Payoff	First Run	______	______
	Second Run	______	______
Fourth Guess / Payoff	First Run	______	______
	Second Run	______	______

Computer Activity III

THREE-DICE GAME

OVERVIEW

This activity is included as an optional exploration for more advanced students. It in essence repeats Computer Activities I and II, using the sums of three dice. Its purpose is to extend and reinforce the ideas and student goals outlined in the two preceding computer activities.

Materials

Microcomputer(s)
Programs—DICE TOSS; DICE GAME.

Worksheets

CIII-1, Three Dice.
CIII-2, Three-Dice Results.
CIII-3, Three-Dice Game.

Computer Activity III
Launch

THREE-DICE GAME

TEACHER ACTION	TEACHER TALK	EXPECTED RESPONSE
You will need Worksheet CIII-1, Three Dice; Worksheet CIII-2, Three-Dice Results; and Worksheet CIII-3, Three-Dice Game.	We have analyzed tossing two dice and looking at the sum.	
	Now we're going to toss three dice. What are the possible sums we might get?	3, 4, 5, 6, . . . 18.
Make a list as students suggest combination.	How many ways could three dice give a sum of 6?	1, 2, 3; 3, 2, 1; 2, 2, 2; 4, 1, 1; 1, 4, 1; 1, 1, 4; etc.

Die 1	Die 2	Die 3
1	2	3
2	2	2
4	1	1
1	4	1
1	1	4
1	3	2
2	1	3
2	3	2
3	1	2
3	2	1

TEACHER ACTION	TEACHER TALK	EXPECTED RESPONSE
Have computer with DICE TOSS loaded.	We found ten different ways to find a sum of 6, but it was hard to find them all, and 6 is only one of the 16 different sums possible. Let's use the computer to simulate tossing three dice. If we ask the computer for 1,000 tosses, the data may be good enough to give us an idea of what the distribution of the sums for three dice looks like. (For *two* dice 1,000 tosses were certainly good enough.)	
Run DICE TOSS.	First we'll run DICE TOSS for three dice, with 1,000 tosses. This will take the computer a couple of minutes.	
	Copy the results on Worksheet CIII-1. Compute the decimal equivalents (percentages). Make the histogram (bar graph).	
	Answer the game questions on Worksheet CIII-2.	

Computer Activity III
Launch

TEACHER ACTION	TEACHER TALK	EXPECTED RESPONSE
	After you have organized your data, run DICE GAME and have the computer make a game for you.	
	Run DICE GAME; this time for three dice. Copy the rules of your game.	
	Look at your data for 1,000 tosses.	
	Decide how many times you would have won.	
	How many times would the computer have won?	
	Try to get a good starting guess at the fair payoff.	
	Then do as you did for the game with two dice: Keep adjusting and running until you're sure you have the best guess for a fair payoff.	

Computer Activity III
Summarize

TEACHER ACTION	TEACHER TALK	EXPECTED RESPONSE
Direct the analysis of the games.	To analyze the three dice games theoretically we need to count the number of ways that we can get each of the sums 3 through 18.	
	We can use our results from two dice and simply match the third dice with each possible sum from two dice.	
Illustrate:	This table shows the sums we can get by taking all sums for two dice and adding in the third.	
	Now we must remember how many ways we could get each sum for two dice. We could get a sum of two in only 1 way so each sum in row one of the table can be gotten in only one way, but those in row two can all be gotten in two ways because the 3 from two dice could be gotten in two ways.	
	I will add the numbers in the table to show how many ways we can get each sum.	

2 dice sums	Third die 1	2	3	4	5	6
2	3	4	5	6	7	8
3	4	5	6	7	8	9
4	5	6	7	8	9	10
5	6	7	8	9	10	11
6	7	8	9	10	11	12
7	8	9	10	11	12	13
8	9	10	11	12	13	14
9	10	11	12	13	14	15
11	11	12	13	14	15	16
11	12	13	14	15	16	17
12	13	14	15	16	17	18

Computer Activity III
Summarize

TEACHER ACTION	TEACHER TALK	EXPECTED RESPONSE
	Now to see how many ways we can roll an 8 with three dice we add all the numbers of ways indicated on each 8 in the table:	
Number of ways to get result on die	6 + 5 + 4 + 3 + 2 + 1 = 21 ways	

→		1	1	1	1	1	1
↓	2 dice sums	Third die 1	2	3	4	5	6
1	2	3①	4①	5①	6①	7①	8①
2	3	4②	5②	6②	7②	8②	9②
3	4	5③	6③	7③	8③	9③	10③
4	5	6④	7④	8④	9④	10④	11④
5	6	7⑤	8⑤	9⑤	10⑤	11⑤	12⑤
6	7	8⑥	9⑥	10⑥	11⑥	12⑥	13⑥
5	8	9⑤	10⑤	11⑤	12⑤	13⑤	14⑤
4	9	10④	11④	12④	13④	14④	15④
3	11	11③	12③	13③	14③	15③	16③
2	11	12②	13②	14②	15②	16②	17②
1	12	13①	14①	15①	16①	17①	18①

TEACHER ACTION	TEACHER TALK	EXPECTED RESPONSE
The following list shows all the possible results.	Now we can use this theoretical model to calculate a fair payoff.	
Illustrate.	Add the numbers next to each sum that gives the computer a win. For example, if the computer wins for 3, 10, 15, 16, add $1 + 27 + 10 + 6 = 44$. Call this sum S.	
	The quantity $\frac{S \times 100}{(216 - S)}$ is the fair payoff.	
	What is the fair payoff?	$\frac{4400}{216 - 44} = \frac{4400}{172} = 25.58$
	We can see how close your experimental guesses were to the theoretical payoff for your game.	

Sum — Number of ways sum can occur

3 – 1
4 – 3
5 – 6
6 – 10
7 – 15
8 – 21
9 – 25
10 – 27
11 – 27
12 – 25
13 – 21
14 – 15
15 – 10
16 – 6
17 – 3
18 – 1

Total: There are 216 ways that three dice can land when tossed.

Illustrate for several group games.

NAME ____________________

Three Dice

List the possible totals for three dice. Then run 1,000 tosses of three dice on the computer. Copy the frequencies. Convert to decimal equivalents or percents, and then graph.

1,000 Tosses—Experiment

Possible Sums																
Number of Occurrences																
Decimal Equivalents																

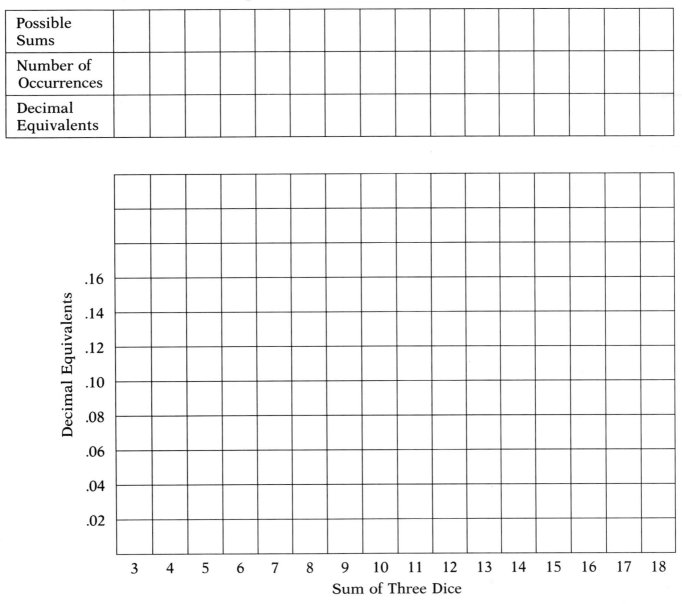

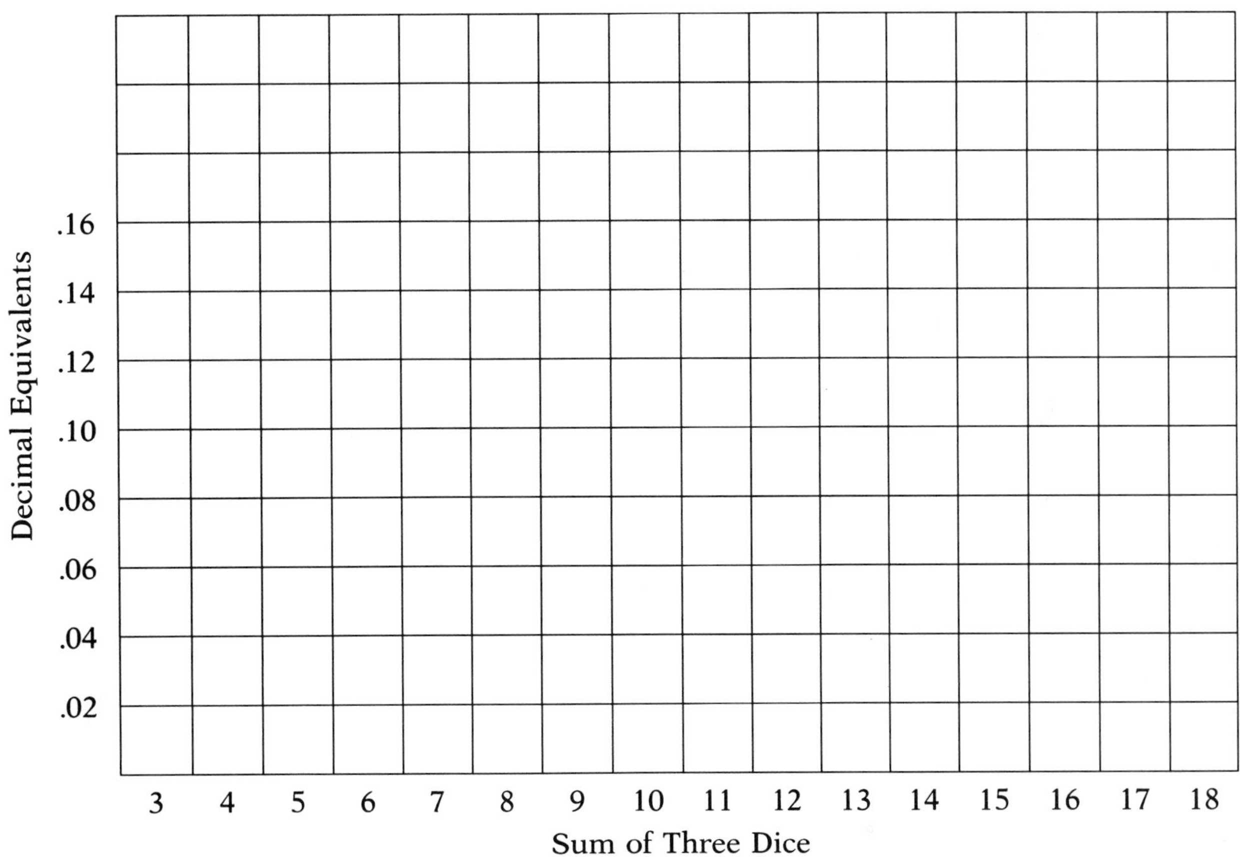

NAME ____________________

Three-Dice Results

Use your data from Worksheet CIII-1 to answer these questions.

Which occurred more frequently, 7 or 9? ________

Which occurred more frequently, 8 or 10? ________

Suppose you had won $1 each time a 3 or an 18 was rolled, but lost a penny each time the total was not 3 or 18. Look at your totals. Figure out how much you would have won and how much you would have lost.

Winnings ____________

Losses ____________

Net Gain ____________ (Winnings minus losses)

Suppose you won 10¢ each time a 10, 11, or 12 came up, but other times you lost a nickel. Look at your totals and record the results.

Winnings ____________

Losses ____________

Net Gain ____________

NAME ______________________

Three-Dice Game

You will need Worksheet CIII-1.
Go to the computer and run the program DICE GAME for three dice.
The computer will design a game just for you.
Write down the rules in the space below.

Computer scores 100 points if sum is: ______________________

You score if the sum is: ______________________

Pretend you have been playing this game for 100 tosses.
Use Worksheet CIII-1 to see how many times you and the computer scored.

Computer scored ________ times.

You scored ________ times.

Computer points scored = ________.

Find a payoff so that your total points are about the same as the computer's. ______
Enter your first guess and run the game twice for 500 tosses each time.

		Your winnings	Computer winnings
First Guess ______ Payoff	First Run	________	________
	Second Run	________	________
Second Guess ______ Payoff	First Run	________	________
	Second Run	________	________
Third Guess ______ Payoff	First Run	________	________
	Second Run	________	________
Fourth Guess ______ Payoff	First Run	________	________
	Second Run	________	________

Materials CIII-1

Dice Toss

```
]LIST

1  REM  DICE ROLLING PROGRAM
3  TEXT : CLEAR : HOME
4  DIM C(18)
8  PRINT : HOME : PRINT: PRINT
9  PRINT "THIS IS A PROGRAM WHICH SIMULATES"
10 X =  RND ( -  PEEK (78) - 256 * PEEK (79))
15  PRINT "ROLLING TWO OR THREE DICE.": PRINT : PRINT
16  INPUT "HOW MANY DICE? ";ND
17  IF ND <  > 2 AND ND <  > 3 THEN 16
18  INPUT "HOW MANY DICE ROLLS WOULD YOU LIKE  ?  ENTER NUMBER AND
     PRESS 'RETURN' . ";B
19 AA = ND:BB = 6 * ND
20  FOR CT = 1 TO B
30 X =  INT ( RND (1) * 6) + 1
40 Y =  INT  ( RND (1) * 6) + 1
45 XX =   INT ( RND (1) * 6) + 1
50 R = X + Y + XX
55  IF ND = 2 THEN R = R - XX
60 C(R) = C(R) + 1
70  NEXT CT
75  PRINT : PRINT "DICE #  NUMBER    PER CENT"
77  PRINT
80  FOR K = AA TO BB
95  PRINT K,C(K),  INT ((C(K) + .005)  / B * 1000) / 10
100  NEXT K
102  PRINT : PRINT
104  PRINT "WHEN YOU ARE READY TO SEE A GRAPH OF  "
106  PRINT "THIS, PRESS ANY KEY."
110  GET J$
120  DIM L(18)
130  FOR K = AA TO BB
140 L(K) =  INT (C(K) / B * 100)
160  NEXT K
170  GR
171  COLOR= 1: FOR DS = 0 to 39
172  HLIN 0,39 AT DS
173  NEXT DS
175  COLOR= 2: GOTO 180
180 XM = 0: FOR ZZ = AA TO BB: IF L(ZZ) > XM THEN XM = L(ZZ)
183  NEXT ZZ
185  IF XM > 19 THEN 200
190  FOR ZZ = AA TO BB:L(ZZ) = 2 * L(ZZ): NEXT ZZ
200  FOR W = AA TO BB
```

```
220   COLOR= W - 2: IF W = 3 THEN COLOR= 9
225   IF L(W) > 39 THEN  LET L(W) = 39
230   IF L(W) = 0 THEN  GOTO 300
250   VLIN 39,39 - L(W) AT (W * 2) - 4
260   VLIN 39,39 - L(W) AT (W * 2 + 1) - 4
300   NEXT W
350   PRINT " 2 3 4 5 6 7 8 9 1 1 1 1 1 1 1 1 "
352   PRINT "                 0 1 2 3 4 5 6 7 8"
365   PRINT "THIS IS A GRAPH OF ";: FLASH : PRINT B" ROLLS.": NORMAL
370   INPUT "HOW ABOUT ANOTHER PROBLEM (Y/N)  ?";U$
380   IF U$ = "Y" THEN 3
390   IF U$ = "N" THEN 400
391   PRINT "PLEASE TYPE EITHER A 'Y' OR AN 'N' .": PRINT : PRINT
392   GOTO 370
400   TEXT : HOME
420   PRINT "IF YOU CHOOSE TO SEE ANOTHER PROBLEM, "
430   PRINT "TYPE 'RUN' AND HIT 'RETURN'."
999   END
1000  TEXT : HOME : LIST
```

Dice Game

```
]LIST

40 X =  RND ( -  PEEK (78) - 256 *  PEEK (79))
50  HOME
55  VTAB 10: HTAB 15: INVERSE : PRINT "DICE GAME": NORMAL
60  VTAB 15: PRINT " IN WHICH YOU AND I PLAY  A GAME OF DICE"
99  FOR I = 1 to 1900: NEXT
100  REM   DICE GAME
110  REM  PROGRAM BY M.J.WINTER
120  REM  FOR MIDDLE GRADES MATH PROJECT
130  REM  MICHIGAN STATE UNIVERSITY
140  REM  EAST LANSING, MI 48824
200  HOME
210  PRINT "WE ARE GOING TO PLAY A GAME WITH DICE."
220  FOR I = 1 to 1999: NEXT I
230  PRINT : PRINT "I AM GOING TO MAKE UP MOST OF THE RULES."
235  FOR I = 1 to 1999: NEXT I
240  PRINT : PRINT "YOUR ASSIGNMENT IS TO MAKE THE GAME FAIR"
250  FOR I = 1 TO 1999: NEXT I
260  PRINT : PRINT "YOU WILL DECIDE ";: INVERSE : PRINT "HOW MUCH";:
     NORMAL : PRINT " YOU WIN"
270  PRINT : PRINT "EACH TIME YOU DO WIN."
280  FOR I = 1 TO 2500: NEXT I
285  PRINT : PRINT
290  INPUT "HOW MANY DICE - 2 or 3  ";DD
300  DIM T(18,2): REM  T(I,2) = 216*FREQ OF I
310  DEF  FN R(X) =  INT (6 *  RND (0) + 1)
320 B$ = "                           "
330  FOR J = 3 TO 18:T(J,1) = 0; READ T(J,2): NEXT J
340  DATA  1,3,6,10,15,21,25,27,27,25,21,15,10,6,3,1
350  RESTORE
360  REM  DESIGN GAME
370 NW = 5 -  INT (3 *  RND (0))
380  FOR J = 1 TO NW
390 X =  RND (1) * (6 * DD - 2) + DD
400 X =  INT (X)
410  IF T(X,1) = 1 THEN 390
420 T(X,1) = 1
430  NEXT J
440  GOTO 1000
500  REM  ENTER OLD GAME
510  DIM T(18,2)
520  DEF  FN R(X) =  INT (6 *  RND (1) + 1)
530 B$ = "                           "
```

```
540  FOR J = 3 TO 18: READ T(J,2): NEXT J
550  RESTORE
560  FOR J = 0 TO 18;T(J,1) = 0: NEXT J
570  PRINT "YOU SET THE RULES THIS TIME"
580  PRINT : INPUT "HOW MANY DICE, 2 OR 3?   ";DD
590  IF DD <  > 2 and DD <  > 3 THEN 580
600  PRINT : PRINT "TYPE IN THE VALUES FOR WHICH I WIN"
610  PRINT "SEPARATE THE VALUES BY STARS *"
620  PRINT : PRINT "IF I WIN ON 12 OR 6 OR 5, ENTER"
630  PRINT "12*6*5"
640  PRINT : INPUT W$
650  IF  LEN (W$) < 3 THEN 600
660 LG =  LEN (W$)
670 V$ = ""
680 X =  VAL (W$):T(X,1) = 1
690 W$ =  MID$ (W$, LEN ( STR$ (X)) + 2)
700  IF  VAL (W$) = 0 THEN 750
705  GOTO 680
710  PRINT
750  PRINT : PRINT "LET'S CHECK"
760  PRINT : PRINT "I WIN ONLY IF THE TOTAL IS:"
770  FOR I = DD TO 6 * DD: IF T(I,1) = 1 THEN  PRINT I;"  ";
775  NEXT I
780  PRINT
790  PRINT "IS THIS CORRECT? PRESS Y OR N"
800  GET A$: IF A$ <  > "Y" AND A$ <  > "N" THEN 800
810  IF A$ = Y THEN 1000
820  FOR I = DD TO 6 * DD:T(I,1) = 0: NEXT I
830  GOTO 600
1000  HOME
1010  PRINT "THESE ARE THE RULES"
1020  PRINT "-------------------------------------"
1025  FOR I = 1 TO 1999: NEXT I
1030  PRINT "I WIN IF THE TOTAL IS:"
1040  FOR J = DD TO 6 * DD
1042  IF T(J,1) = 1 THEN  PRINT J;" ";:
1044  NEXT J
1050  PRINT
1060  PRINT : PRINT " YOU WIN IF THE TOTAL IS:"
1070  FOR J = DD TO 6 * DD
1072  IF T(J,1) = 0 THEN  PRINT J;"  ";
1074  NEXT J
1080  PRINT : PRINT "-------------------------------------"
1100 K = 0
1110 MP = 100
```

```
1120  FOR I = 1 TO 1999: NEXT I
1130  PRINT : PRINT "WHEN I WIN, I GET "MP" POINTS"
1140  PRINT "WE WANT THIS GAME TO BE ";: INVERSE : PRINT "FAIR":
      NORMAL
1150  PRINT : PRINT "HOW MANY POINTS SHOULD YOU GET WHEN"
1155  INVERSE : PRINT "YOU";: NORMAL : PRINT " WIN?"
1160  INPUT YP
1170  PRINT "OK, WE'LL PLAY 500 GAMES"
1180  PRINT : PRINT "PRESS B TO BEGIN"
1190  GET A$: IF A$ <  > "B" THEN 1190
1200  HOME
1210  PRINT "I WIN ";MP;" POINTS IF THE TOTAL IS"
1220  FOR J = DD TO 6 * DD: IF T(J,1) = 1 THEN  PRINT J;" ";:
1222  NEXT J
1230  PRINT : PRINT : PRINT "YOU WIN ";YP;" POINTS IF THE TOTAL IS"
1240  FOR J = DD TO 6 * DD: IF T(J,1) = 0 THEN PRINT J;"  ";
1242  NEXT J
1250  PRINT
1260  PRINT "-------------------------------------"
1280  VTAB 14: PRINT "GAME";: HTAB 12: PRINT "YOUR SCORE";: HTAB 24:
      PRINT "MY SCORE"
1290 MS = 0:YS = 0
1300  FOR G = 1 TO 500
1310 T =  INT (6 *  RND (1) + 1) +  INT (6 *  RND (1) + 1)
1312  IF DD = 3 THEN T = T +  INT (6 *  RND (0) + 1)
1320  IF T(T,1) = 1 THEN MS = MS + MP
1330  IF T(T,1) = 0 THEN YS = YS + YP
1350  VTAB 16: PRINT G;: HTAB 12: PRINT YS;: HTAB 24: PRINT MS
1400  NEXT G
1410  PRINT "----------------------------------"
1450  FOR I = 1 TO 1000: NEXT I
1460  VTAB 19: PRINT "DO YOU THINK THIS GAME WAS FAIR?"
1470  PRINT "PRESS Y OR N"
1480  GET A$: IF A$ <  > "N" AND A$ <  > "Y" THEN 1480
1490  IF A$ = "N" THEN 1000
1500  IF A$ = "Y" THEN PRINT "WOULD YOU LIKE TO PLAY ANOTHER ROUND"
1510  PRINT "TO MAKE SURE?"
1520  GET A$: IF A$ <  > "Y" AND A$ <  > "N" THEN 1520
1530  IF A$ = "Y" THEN 1200
1540  PRINT "TO RE-ENTER A GAME, TYPE RUN 500"; END
2000 X = 3
2010 S$ =  STR$ (X)
2020  PRINT S$
2030 W$ = "12*2*4"
2040  PRINT  VAL (W$)
```

Activity 4

FAIR AND UNFAIR GAMES III

OVERVIEW

In this activity, fair and unfair games are extended to games involving a Game board and to games that involve spinners (area). The Hare and the Tortoise Game is based on tossing a pair of dice three times and looking at the outcomes even/odd. There are eight outcomes: OOO, OOE, OEO, EOO, EEO, OEE, EOE, EEE. The hare is given five positions on which to score, the tortoise only two. In the beginning, most students will think the game favors the hare. However, the hare will win on only two outcomes of the dice, EEE and OOO, because three of the five positions turn out to be impossible to land on. The tortoise is given two positions on which to score and can land on both of these positions, depending on which of the six remaining outcomes of the dice turn up.

The second part of this activity introduces the idea of area (such as a spinner) representing probabilities. Various circles are partitioned into parts and labeled A, B, C, D, etc. The students must experimentally determine the probability of the spinner stopping in a given region. Bobby pins and pencils are recommended as spinners. They are extremely easy to use and give excellent results. The experimental probabilities are compared to the theoretical by analyzing the relationship of the area of each region to the whole circle. For example,

in [B A], P(A) $= \frac{3}{4}$ and P(B) $= \frac{1}{4}$. In [D A B A D C] the denominator of the theoretical probability is 8 and P(A) $= \frac{2}{8}$. The fractions are renamed using 96 as a denominator because $\frac{24}{96}$ is easier to compare to the experimental probabilities that have 100 as a denominator. For younger students it suffices to say that $\frac{27}{100}$ is quite close to $\frac{24}{96}$.

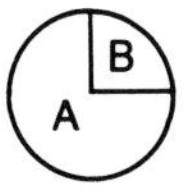

Area models to represent probabilities are a convenient way to analyze probabilities in more complicated situations, as in Activities 6, 7, and 8, where successive choices must be made or where the second event *depends* upon the first event.

Goals for students

1. Collect and analyze data.
2. Determine experimental probabilities.
2. Determine theoretical probabilities.
3. Compare experimental and theoretical probabilities.
4. Make a fair game based on known probabilities.

Materials

30 dice.

30 bobby pins (used for markers and as spinners); paper clips can be used in place of bobby pins.

Worksheets

*4-1, The Hare and the Tortoise Game.

*4-2, Spinners.

Transparencies

Starred items should be made into transparencies.

FAIR AND UNFAIR GAMES III

TEACHER ACTION	TEACHER TALK	EXPECTED RESPONSE
Pass out Worksheet 4-1, The Hare and Tortoise Game. Describe the Hare and the Tortoise Game. Draw the game board on the board or display on a transparency. 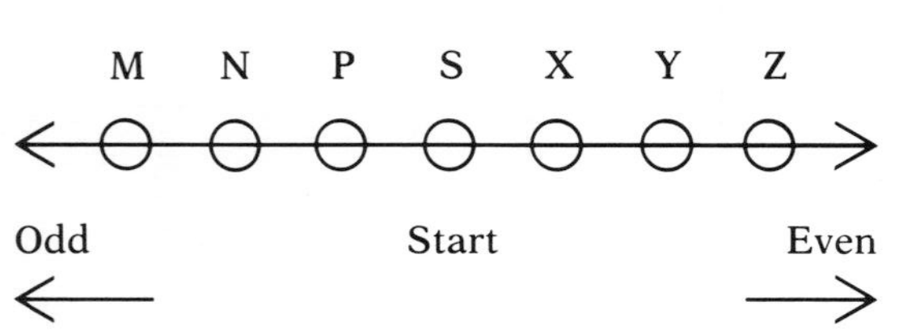 	The game rules for the Hare and the Tortoise Game: 1. The tortoise and the hare start *each turn* at S. 2. Each turn consists of three moves. The player will roll a die a total of three times on each turn. After each roll the player's marker is moved one place to the left if the number on the die is odd and one place to the right if the number on the die is even. 3. Scoring: The tortoise gets a point if at the end of the three moves the marker is on position P or X. The hare gets a point if the marker ends at position M, N, S, Y or Z. 4. Players alternate turns until *each* has had 16 turns. 5. To start play: Each player rolls a die. The highest number chooses a character, hare or tortoise, and takes the first turn.	
Ask.	Is this a fair game?	Most students will think it is unfair.
	Who does the game favor?	It favors the hare because the hare can land on more points than the tortoise.
Take one or two turns to show the class how to play the game.		
Divide the class into pairs. Allow about 5 minutes to play the game.		

OBSERVATIONS	POSSIBLE RESPONSES
There may be some confusion on how to tally.	Check to make sure each pair is playing and recording correctly. Students must record a mark for each complete play whether or not a point is awarded for that play. For example, if on the hare's turn the marker lands on P a tally mark for P must be recorded in the hare's column. When the game is done, students will mark the total points, the hare counting only M, N, S, Y, and Z and the tortoise counting only P and X.
Students will be surprised to see that the game is not fair because of who it favors.	
Many students will discover that S, N, and Y are impossible to land on.	Ask students to give reasons to support their observations. Suggest that advanced students try flipping a penny and using heads or tails instead of odd or even. Will this make a difference? Get students thinking about how the game could be fair. What are the total outcomes, etc? Make up a game board for four pennies or four rolls of the die. Make up rules such that each position has a chance of being used.

TEACHER ACTION	TEACHER TALK	EXPECTED RESPONSE
Ask.	Were you surprised by the results?	Yes!
	Is this a fair game? Why?	No; it favors the tortoise.
Display a transparency of Worksheet 4-1 and collect data from class.		
Ask.	What probabilities do we get from our class data?	Answers should be close to the following. $P(Z) = \frac{1}{8}$ $P(M) = \frac{1}{8}$ $P(X) = \frac{3}{8}$ $P(P) = \frac{3}{8}$ $P(N) = P(Y) = P(S) = 0$
	Did the play end at all points?	No; it is impossible to end at N and Y.

Explain. Elicit plays from the class and put them on the board as follows:

E = Even O = Odd

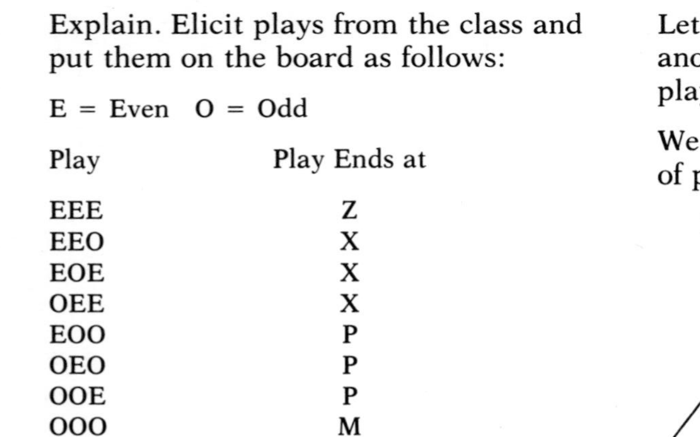

Play	Play Ends at
EEE	Z
EEO	X
EOE	X
OEE	X
EOO	P
OEO	P
OOE	P
OOO	M

List these outcomes at the positions on the game board.

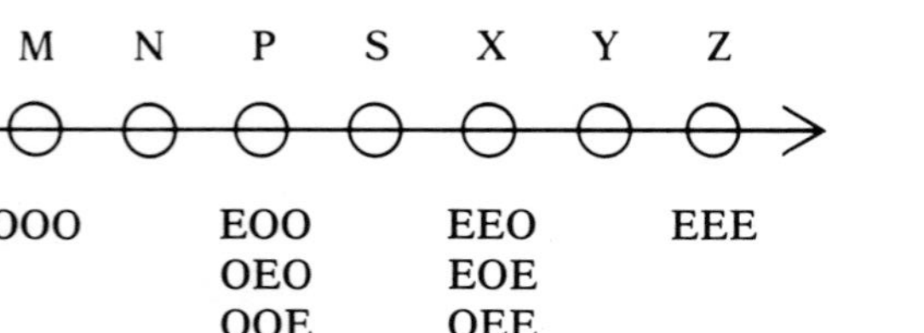

Let's see if we can analyze this game another way. Let's list all the possible plays.

We could also see this by making a tree of possible positions.

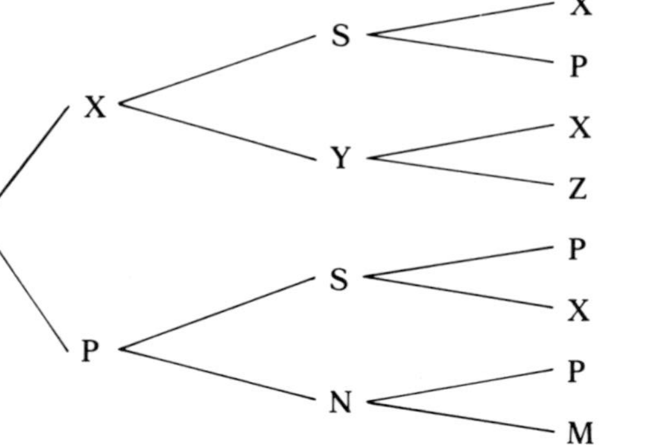

TEACHER ACTION	TEACHER TALK	EXPECTED RESPONSE
Ask.	How many possible plays are there?	8
	How many plays end at X?	3
	How many plays end at P?	3
	How many plays end at Z?	1
	How many plays end at M?	1
	How many end at N, S and Y?	0
	What is the probability that the tortoise wins? What is the probability that the hare wins?	Tortoise: P(win) $= \frac{6}{8} = \frac{3}{4}$ Hare: P(win) $= \frac{2}{8} = \frac{1}{4}$
	How can we make this a fair game?	Change the points; for example, give the hare three points for a win. Change the rules; for example, let the hare win if it lands on M and P, and the tortoise win if it lands on X and Z.
Compare the above results to tossing three pennies on Worksheet 2-2. Students will see the similarity quickly if the three penny games were analyzed in class.		
Illustrate as in the table below.		

Possible Plays	Outcome for Three Pennies
EEE	HHH
EEO	HHT
EOE	HTH
OEE	THH
EOO	HTT
OEO	THT
OOE	TTH
OOO	TTT

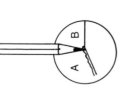

TEACHER ACTION	TEACHER TALK	EXPECTED RESPONSE
Display a transparency of Worksheet 4-2. Explore the first game board.		
Explain.	Many games involve spinners. We are going to investigate how the areas marked on the spinner circles relate to the probability that the spinner will land in that area.	
Spin spinner 1 a couple of times. Show students how to use the pencil and bobby pin for spinners. Use pencil point to hold bobby pin in position.	How should I spin the spinner to make sure my results are fair (random)?	Various answers.
	How often will the spinner land in area A?	Various answers. $\frac{3}{4}$, 75%, more than half the time, etc.
Pass out Worksheet 4-2, Spinners, and bobby pins for the spinner. You may want to change the number of spins; the total number of spins should be multiples of 100 to make it easier to determine experimental probabilities.	To see how good our guess is, spin each pair 100 times and record what happens. Then we will collect class data.	
	Each pair will gather data for 100 spins on spinner 1. In addition, each pair will be assigned one of the remaining two spinners and gather data on it.	
Assign number 2 and number 3 so that several pairs are working with each spinner.		

Activity 4 *Explore*

OBSERVATIONS	POSSIBLE RESPONSES
	Make sure students are randomly spinning their spinners. Suggest they change or vary their spinning techniques.

Activity 4 *Summarize*

TEACHER ACTION | **TEACHER TALK** | **EXPECTED RESPONSE**

Collect probabilities from each group and list the data on the overhead one spinner at a time.

Spinner 1

Group	1	2	3	4	5
P(A)					
P(B)					

Teacher talk: When I call on your group, give the probabilities for spinner 1.

Spinner 2

Group	1	2	3	4	5
P(A)					
P(B)					
P(C)					
P(D)					

Teacher talk: When I call on your group, give the probabilities for spinner 2.

TEACHER ACTION	TEACHER TALK	EXPECTED RESPONSE
Spinner 3	When I call on your group, give the probabilities for spinner 3.	

Group	1	2	3	4	5
P(A)					
P(B)					
P(C)					
P(D)					

Discuss reasons for any large difference between groups. Compare small group probabilities to the total results.

TEACHER ACTION	TEACHER TALK	EXPECTED RESPONSE
	To see if these experimental results are what we would expect let's analyze each spinner and assign theoretical probabilities.	
	What part of the circle in spinner 1 is marked B?	$\frac{1}{4}$
	What part is marked A?	$\frac{3}{4}$
If students do not see this quickly, draw in lines on the spinner to show the four equal areas.	So we would have expected the spinner to stop in area B about $\frac{1}{4}$ of the time and in area A about $\frac{3}{4}$ of the time.	
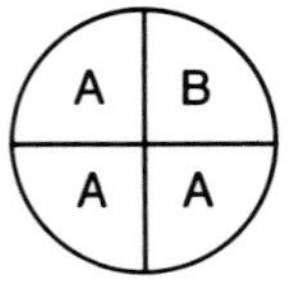	Since we spun 100 times we need to write $\frac{1}{4}$ as a fraction with 100 in the denominator.	
	How can we do this?	$\frac{1}{4} = \frac{25}{100}$
	How about $\frac{3}{4}$?	$\frac{3}{4} = \frac{75}{100}$
Look back at the group reports one by one and compare them to $\frac{25}{100}$ and $\frac{75}{100}$. Usually they will be very close.	Now let's look at the data reported and see how close the groups came to our theoretical results.	

TEACHER ACTION	TEACHER TALK	EXPECTED RESPONSE
	Now let's analyze spinner 2. What line segment could we draw in to make our analysis easier?	A line splitting D and C.
	Now what is P(A)?	$\frac{2}{8}$
	Now what is P(B)?	$\frac{1}{8}$
	What is P(C)?	$\frac{2}{8}$
	What is P(D)?	$\frac{3}{8}$
Explain. If you prefer, convert these results to decimals and then compare the theoretical and experimental probabilities.	To help us compare our experimental and theoretical probabilities, rename $\frac{2}{8}$ as an equivalent fraction with a larger denominator. Multiply by $\frac{12}{12}$ to make the denominator quite close to 100.	$\frac{2}{8} \times \frac{12}{12} = \frac{24}{96}$
	Let's rename the other probabilities.	
	Rename P(B) or $\frac{1}{8}$.	$P(B) = \frac{12}{96}$
	Rename P(C) or $\frac{2}{8}$.	$P(C) = \frac{24}{96}$
	Rename P(D) or $\frac{3}{8}$.	$P(D) = \frac{36}{96}$
Compare the probabilities to see how good the group data is.	We can use these values to get approximate test results for our experiment, since 96 is very close to 100.	

TEACHER ACTION	TEACHER TALK	EXPECTED RESPONSE
	Spinner 3 needs several lines drawn in to help our analysis. What lines do you suggest?	Various answers.
Take all responses until you have the circle partitioned into 16 congruent parts. 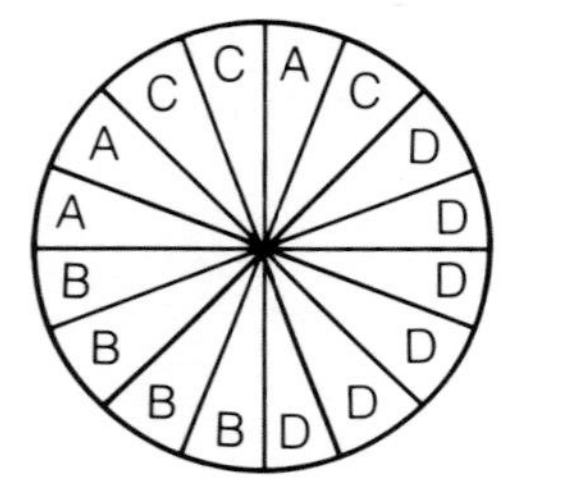	Now what is P(A)?	$P(A) = \frac{3}{16}$
	What is P(B)?	$P(B) = \frac{4}{16}$
	What is P(C)?	$P(C) = \frac{3}{16}$
	What is P(D)?	$P(D) = \frac{6}{16}$
Again use decimals if appropriate for your students.	As before, we can rename these fractions with 96 in the denominator to approximate our 100 spins.	
Compare with experimental data. The data usually is quite close to the expected probabilities. If there are differences, you might discuss what they might mean. For example, make the point that probabilities are not guarantees. We can still get very unexpected results even when we have gathered our data fairly. However, we may not be working with a fair spinner or spinning technique.	$P(A) = \frac{3}{16} = \frac{18}{96}$ $P(B) = \frac{4}{16} = \frac{24}{96}$ $P(C) = \frac{3}{16} = \frac{18}{96}$ $P(D) = \frac{6}{16} = \frac{36}{96}$	

NAME ____________________

The Hare and the Tortoise Game

Materials

Game board, a marker (bobby pin), and a die for each player.

Game Rules

1. The tortoise and the hare start *each turn* at S.
2. Each turn consists of three moves. The player will roll a die a total of three times per turn. After each roll, the player's marker is moved one place to the left if the number on the die is odd and one place to the right if the number on the die is even.
3. Scoring: The tortoise gets a point if at the end of the three moves the marker is on position P or X. The hare gets a point if the marker ends at position M, N, S, Y or Z.
4. Players alternate turns until *each* has had 16 turns.
5. To start play: Each player rolls a die. The highest number chooses a character, hare or tortoise, and takes the first turn.

Game Board

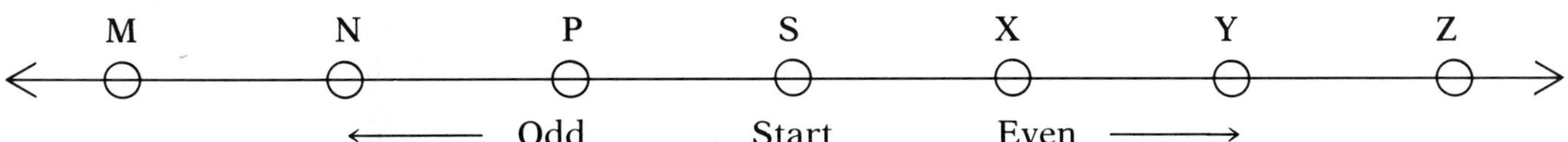

Record Sheet

As you play the game, record where you land at the end of each turn by putting a tally mark in the appropriate space.

Position Play Ends	Hare—16 turns	Tortoise—16 turns	Totals for all 32 turns
P			
X			
M			
N			
S			
Y			
Z			

Hare scored ______ points. Tortoise scored ______ points.

What is the probability that a player ends at position P? P(P) = ______

At position X? P(X) = ______ At position S? P(S) = ______

At position M? P(M) = ______ At position Y? P(Y) = ______

At position N? P(N) = ______ At position Z? P(Z) = ______

NAME ______________________

Spinners

For each spinner, determine the probability of the indicated regions.

1. Spin 100 times.

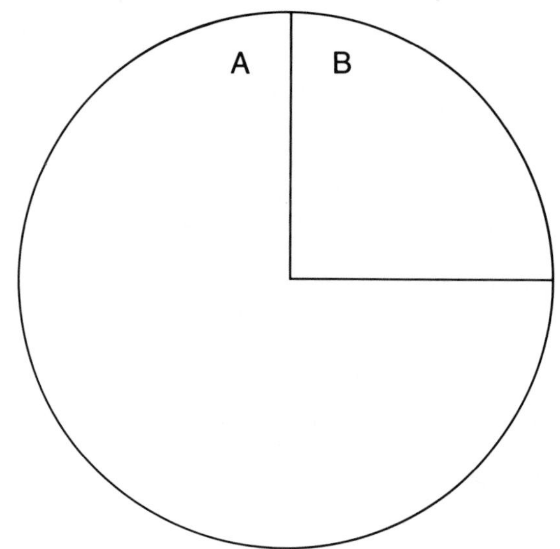

	Tally	Total
A		
B		

P(A) = ________

P(B) = ________

2. Spin 100 times.

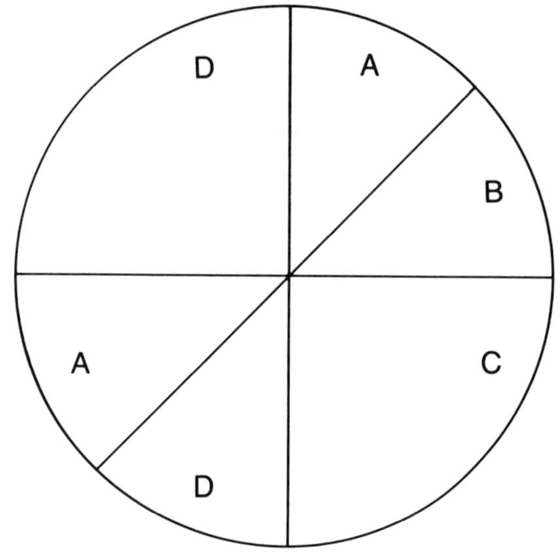

	Tally	Total
A		
B		
C		
D		

P(A) = ________ P(C) = ________

P(B) = ________ P(D) = ________

3. Spin 100 times.

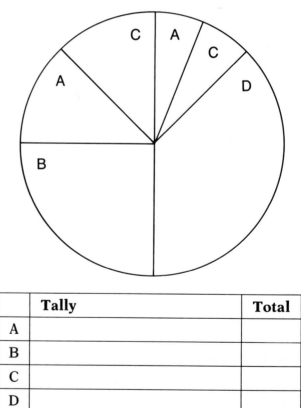

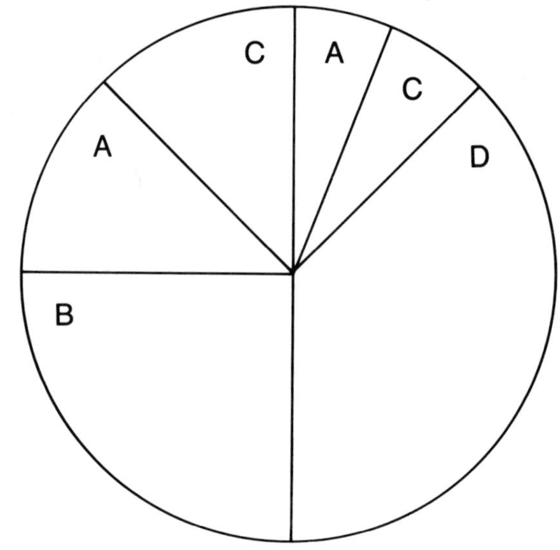

	Tally	Total
A		
B		
C		
D		

P(A) = ________ P(C) = ________

P(B) = ________ P(D) = ________

Activity 5 SURVEYS

OVERVIEW

This activity allows students to explore a very important application of probability: using survey information to make predictions or decisions. It describes just one possible type of survey, that of surveying a small group of students for favorite sports, forming ratios (probabilities), and using this information to decide which sports should be funded for the school and county. Other surveys can be used, such as favorite school lunches to make up menus, traffic patterns, number of bicycle racks needed, voting to predict local or national elections, and predicting weather.

The important thing is to choose a survey that will interest your students. Often a local school or community issue will give rise to a survey topic that is of great interest to the students.

Each of the surveys suggested above can be analyzed in a number of ways, such as girls vs. boys, 6th grade vs. 7th grade, etc.

This is the first time the students have been exposed to situations in which there is no theoretical probability. The best we can do is to gather experimental data carefully and assume that it reflects the true proportions in the population.

Goals for students

1. Conduct a survey.
2. Collect data and tabulate.
3. Compute ratios.
4. Derive experimental probabilities.
5. Make predictions.
6. Conduct a second survey to check predictions.
7. Understand that surveys show tendencies, not exact results.
8. Analyze what factors may cause experimental data to be a poor predictor.

Materials

Plain paper to use as ballots.

Sports ballots with six sports listed on each and a survey question to be asked.

Worksheets

5-1, Experimental Probabilities.

SURVEYS

TEACHER ACTION	TEACHER TALK	EXPECTED RESPONSE
Explain. If students have been bringing in articles on how probabilities have been used, look for one which involves a survey. Use it in your explanation.	One of the ways in which probability is used is to gain information from a small sample and use the information to predict what an entire population will do. For example, I am the cook at school, and I want to know what the favorite vegetable is. I go out in the hall and ask three students, "What is your favorite vegetable?" Answer: 1 peas and 2 corn. On the basis of this answer, I will serve corn twice as often as peas. Is this a good idea? Why?	Various answers; try to get opinions and reasons supporting yes and no.
Tell a story. (You should alter the list of sports to fit your situation and students.)	A county board is trying to cut back on the money allotted to schools. One of the items they are thinking about cutting back on is athletics in grades 5–8. At present they support baseball, hockey, basketball, football, volleyball and soccer. Before cutting out any of these sports, the board decides to take a poll of this class to find out which sports students like best. On the basis of this poll, the board will make its decision for the entire county.	
Pass out blank ballots. Write the six sports on the board: Tally / Total Baseball Volleyball Basketball Football Hockey Soccer Total Votes ______ Collect the ballots and tally the votes.	Let's vote and see what happens. Write your favorite sport on the ballot. Vote for only one.	

Activity 5 *Launch*

TEACHER ACTION	TEACHER TALK	EXPECTED RESPONSE
Ask.	What is the favorite sport of this class? What is the second favorite, etc?	Various answers.
	On the basis of this class, if I go out in the hall and ask ten students what their favorite sport is, what can I expect?	Various answers, depending on the class results.
	Would you expect the entire school to vote the way we did?	Check for such things as whether the class is mostly boys or girls, whether the class contains the majority of the football team, etc.
	Would you expect all the schools in the county to vote this way?	No; soccer may be very strong in some schools, for example, but some schools may not have a hockey program.
Be sure to keep the class data for comparison with the school population.	Is this method a fair way of allotting the money?	Allow some discussion; the favorite sport may change from season to season, from school to school.
Pass out the sports ballots for each student to record data.	To see how representative our class is, each student is to ask 3 or 4 students in the school to name their favorite sport.	
Allow one day for collecting data.	What guidelines should we follow to make this as fair as possible?	Don't ask only good friends, only people on your team, only students of one sex, adults, etc.

What is your favorite sport from among these six?

	Student #1	#2	#3	#4
Baseball				
Volleyball				
Basketball				
Football				
Hockey				
Soccer				

Activity 5 *Summarize*

TEACHER ACTION	TEACHER TALK	EXPECTED RESPONSE
Collect data.		
Put results on the board.		
Compute ratios.		
Compare with class ratios.		
Discuss the results. Solicit reasons for any discrepencies.		
Explain.	In this experiment we have *no* theoretical probability with which to compare. Thus, in real life, special attention must be paid to the size and type of the sample population used.	
Ask.	Where else is this type of probability (surveying) used?	Various responses; to determine which products consumers like, TV preferences, candidates, etc.
You may want to have students ask friends in another school to repeat the poll and then to compare data.		
Pass out Worksheet 5-1, Experimental Probabilities.		

NAME ____________________

Experimental Probabilities

1. Select a passage from a book. Count the number of vowels and the total number of letters in the passage. Tabulate your results in the table below.

Vowel	Number Counted	P
a		
e		
i		
o		
u		
Total Letters in the Passage		

Use this probability to predict the number of e's in another passage. Check the passage to see how close your prediction comes to the actual count.

2. A poll was taken of 40 students on their favorite school lunch. The results are below.

Hamburgers and fries	14
Pizza and salad	13
Spaghetti and salad	8
Hot dogs and beans	5
Liver and spinach	0
Total	40

a. If a student is chosen at random, what is the probability that he or she favors

Hamburgers and fries?
Pizza and salad?
Spaghetti and salad?
Hot dogs and beans?
Liver and spinach?

b. If there are 400 students in the school, how many prefer

Hamburgers? Hot dogs? Liver?

c. How can the cook use this information to plan a menu for 20 school days?

NAME ______________________

Experimental Probabilities

3. A poll is taken of 50 students on their opinions of a rule that would prohibit them from riding bikes to school. The results of the poll are tabulated below.

	Students who ride to school on a bike	Students who ride to school in a bus	Students who walk to school	Total
Favor the Rule	1	12	10	23
Oppose the Rule	8	10	4	22
No Opinion	1	3	1	5
Total	10	25	15	50

If a student is chosen at random, what is the probability that he or she

favors the rule?
rides a bus and opposes the rule?
rides a bike or opposes the rule?

4. It has been estimated that in using a calculator, a mistake is made once in every 25 entries. If a certain problem requires 75 entries on the calculator, what is the probability that an error is made?

What is the probability that no error is made?

5. Conduct a poll in your class on one of the following items. Check it with a sample of students outside of your class.

a. What is the favorite color?
b. What is the favorite song?
c. What day of the week has the most absences? (Check results of this one with the school office.)
d. Is tardiness related to distance from school? Break students into groups of bus riders, car riders, one block walkers, two block walkers, etc.

Activity 6

AREA MODELS

OVERVIEW

The first five activities involved determining probabilities of *independent events*. For example, the outcome of one die is independent of the outcome of the second die. In this activity, students are introduced to probabilistic situations in which one event depends on another event.

There are two major parts. The first part involves a maze that starts at a common point but can end in one of two rooms. If paths are chosen randomly, students must decide which room is most likely to be the room in which the maze ends. Ending up in one of the rooms depends upon choosing a succession of paths.

The second part involves selecting a hat and then picking a marble from the hat. The challenge is to arrange two black and two white marbles in the two hats to maximize the probability of drawing a white marble. Drawing a marble out of a hat depends upon first choosing a hat.

In these examples a simple listing of the possible events does not help very much because the outcomes are not equally likely. For instance, in the four marbles in two hats example the students have to find the probability of drawing a white marble in one draw from one of the two hats chosen at random. Suppose the marbles are placed as shown below.

If we tried to calculate P(W) directly, we would have to multiply probabilities and then add probabilities

P(H1 and W) + P(H2 and W)

$$\left(\frac{1}{2} \times \frac{1}{3}\right) + \left(\frac{1}{2} \times 1\right) = \frac{1}{6} + \frac{1}{2} = \frac{4}{6} = \frac{2}{3}$$

This approach is very difficult for most students to understand. That it must be made for all the possible arrangements of the marbles makes this analysis even more confusing. However, using an area model to analyze the situation makes the problem quite accessible to students in grades 6, 7, and 8.

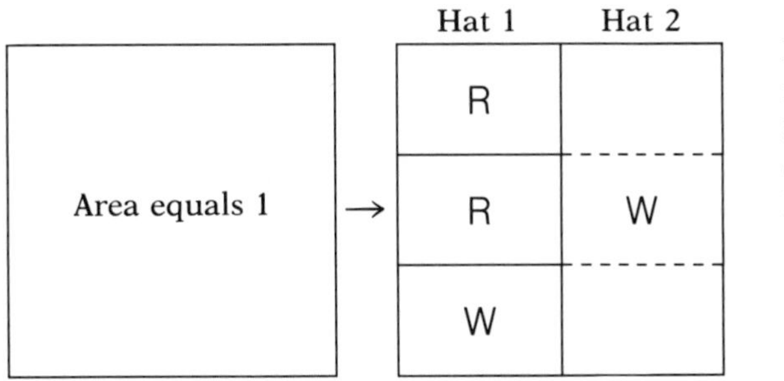

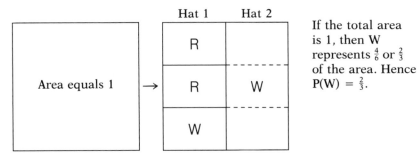

If the total area is 1, then W represents $\frac{4}{6}$ or $\frac{2}{3}$ of the area. Hence $P(W) = \frac{2}{3}$.

This type of analysis is very useful in situations requiring more than one choice to complete an event and the choices available depend on what happened before.

Activity 6

Goals for students

1. Organize data.
2. Understand the phrase "to choose at random."
3. Partition the area of a square so that the parts will represent the probabilities of every possible outcome.
4. Using an area model, analyze a situation to determine theoretical probability.
5. For appropriate grade levels, relate the area model to multiplying probabilities.

Materials

Coin for choosing paths on a maze (optional).

Two colored pencils (for teacher transparency).

Two colored pencils for each student (optional).

*Materials 6-1, The Maze.

*Materials 6-2, Another Maze.

Worksheets

*6-1, Which Is Best?

*6-2, Darts Anyone?

Transparencies

Starred items should be made into transparencies.

TEACHER ACTION	TEACHER TALK	EXPECTED RESPONSE
	The first choice he has to make is between the upper, middle, and lower paths.	
	How should we partition the area of the square to represent the probabilities that should be assigned for this first choice Mr. Green must make?	Partition the area into three equal parts.
Make partitions with two colored pens. Write down the number of squares in each region as you partition. 12 Upper 12 Middle 12 Lower	Let's partition the area with red horizontal lines and label the paths. How many small squares should be in each part?	12
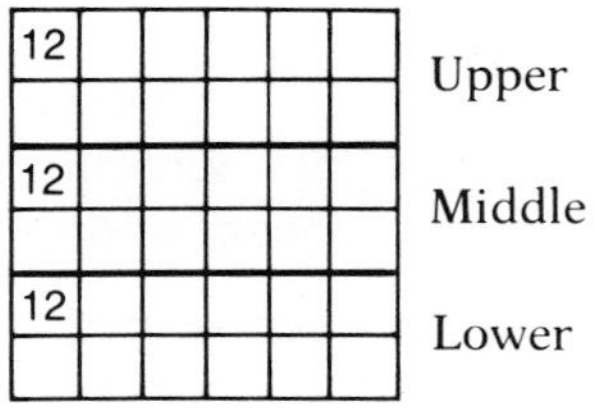 Upper A B	Now let's analyze each path that we have started. First, the upper path splits into two paths, one leading to A and one to B.	
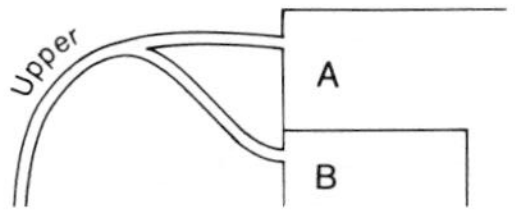	How should we partition the area of the upper path to show this split?	Partition it into two equal areas.
6 A 6 B Upper 12 12	We will use a green vertical line through the area for the upper path to show the split. Let's label each part with the letter of the room to which the path leads.	
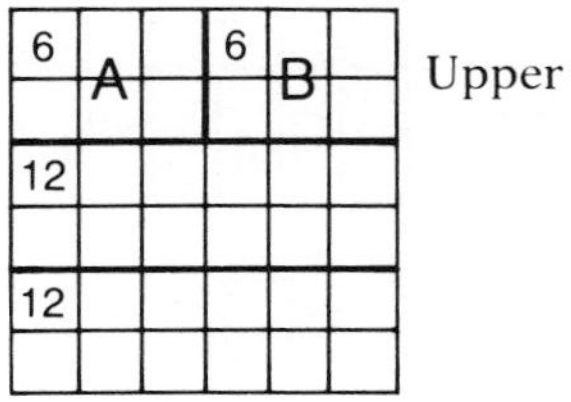	How many squares are in each of the new areas?	6
	In the same way let's analyze the middle and lower paths. Should the middle path be partitioned?	No; it leads only to room B.

TEACHER ACTION	TEACHER TALK	EXPECTED RESPONSE
6 B 6 A Upper 12 B Middle	Then let's label the middle area B.	
	How should we partition the area for the lower path?	We should partition the area into 3 equal parts and mark one B and two A.
Lower B A	How many small squares are in each part?	4
	In all, how many small squares represent ending in room A? How many represent ending in room B?	14 squares for A; 22 squares for B.
6 A 6 B Upper 12 B Middle 4 B 4 A 4 A Lower	How would we express this as a probability?	$P(A) = \frac{14}{36} = \frac{7}{18}$ $P(B) = \frac{22}{36} = \frac{11}{18}$
	Which room are you most likely to enter?	Room B.

Display a transparency of Another Maze (Materials 6-2). Have students vote on which room is most likely to be entered.

Repeat analysis of Mr. Green and the students with a new diagram of the maze.

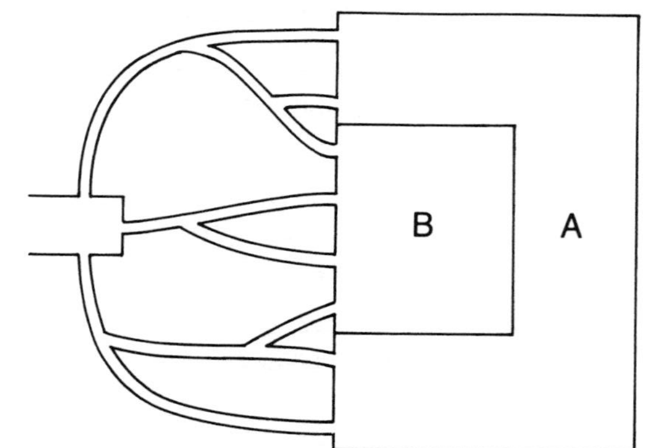

TEACHER ACTION	TEACHER TALK	EXPECTED RESPONSE
3 A 6 A Upper 3 B 12 B Middle 6 A 3 B Lower 3 A	What is the probability that Mr. Green will enter room A? What is the probability that Mr. Green will enter room B?	$P(A) = \frac{18}{36} = \frac{1}{2}$ $P(B) = \frac{18}{36} = \frac{1}{2}$
	In which room should the students place the cookbook?	Either.

TEACHER ACTION	TEACHER TALK	EXPECTED RESPONSE
Tell the story.	Here is another problem to consider.	
	We are given an opportunity to win a prize. We are given two hats and two marbles, one red marble and one white marble. We may arrange the marbles in the hats any way we choose. Then another person will randomly draw one marble out of one of the hats. If the marble is white we'll win the prize. How should we arrange the marbles?	Various answers.
Illustrate. Case 1: H1 (W, R), H2 (empty) Case 2: H1 (W), H2 (R)	Let's list all the possibilities. There are essentially only two.	
	1. Both marbles are in one of the hats.	
	2. One marble is in each hat.	
	We will use an area model to find P(W) in each case.	
Illustrate. Case 1: H1 | H2 → H1: R / W, H2: empty Case 2: H1 | H2 → H1: W, H2: R	First we choose a hat H1 or H2. Each has an equal chance. Then we partition the area for each hat to represent the probability of drawing a red or a white marble from that hat.	
	What is the probability of drawing either the red or white marble in case 1?	$P(R) = \frac{1}{4}$ $P(W) = \frac{1}{4}$
	What is the probability of drawing either the red or white marble in case 2?	$P(R) = \frac{1}{2}$ $P(W) = \frac{1}{2}$
	Which arrangement is the best?	Case 2.

TEACHER ACTION	TEACHER TALK	EXPECTED RESPONSE
Tell a story. Illustrate. Two Hats H1 H2 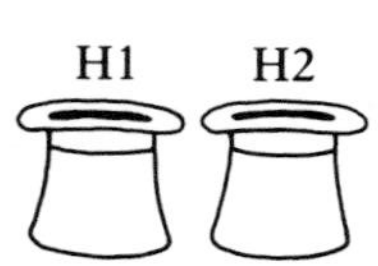 Four marbles R R W W	Now, suppose that you and a friend are given an opportunity to win a prize. You are given two hats and *four marbles.* Two of the marbles are red and two are white. You may put them into the two hats in any way you choose. After you have placed the marbles into the hats, the hats will be taken to your friend, who will reach into one of the hats to pull out a marble. If the marble is white, you and your friend will share the prize. Otherwise, you win nothing. This includes winning nothing if your friend chooses an empty hat. How should you arrange the marbles to optimize your chances of winning the prize?	
Students need Worksheet 6-1, Which Is Best? If possible, provide colored pens for the students to mark areas with so that their work shows on the black grid.	On your worksheet you have several grid squares to use in analyzing this problem. First list every possible way that you could arrange the marbles in the hats.	
Take suggestions from the class until five *different* possibilities are found. 1. 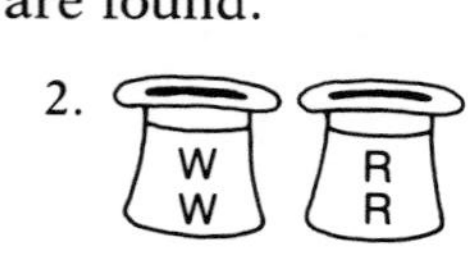 2.  3.  4. W	W R R 5. 	Mark your worksheets as I mark the overhead. Now find the probabilities for each case.	

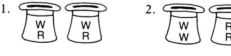

OBSERVATIONS	POSSIBLE RESPONSES
	If a student has trouble getting started, ask what all the possible arrangements are.
	Mark the hats with each arrangement.
	How can we represent the probability of picking a hat?
	In hat 1, how can I represent the probability of picking a red marble? How can I represent the probability of picking a white marble?
	What are all the outcomes (denominator)? The denominator equals the total number of squares.
	How many squares represent red (numerator)?
	Suggest that students add another grid.
A student may claim there are six arrangements by saying	Suggest that more advanced students find the best arrangement for three red and three white marbles. What happens if we add a third hat?
this H1: RW RW, H2: (empty) is different	With two hats W / WW RRR gives $\frac{7}{10}$.
from this H1: (empty), H2: RW RW	With three hats W / W / W RRR gives $\frac{9}{12}$ or $\frac{3}{4}$.

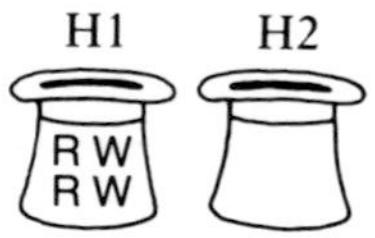

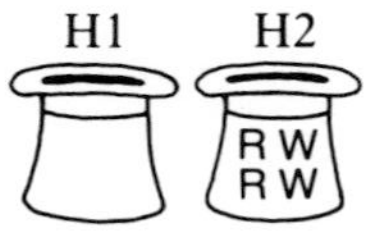

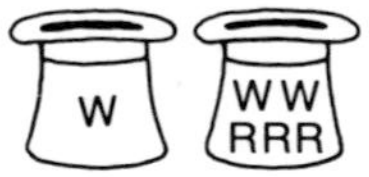

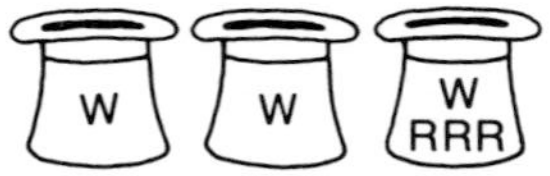

TEACHER ACTION	TEACHER TALK	EXPECTED RESPONSE		
Discuss the results of Worksheet 6-1.	What is the probability of each arrangement?	Hat 1	Hat 2	
		WW		$P(R) = \frac{1}{4}$
		RR		$P(W) = \frac{1}{4}$
		WW	RR	$P(R) = \frac{1}{2}$
				$P(W) = \frac{1}{2}$
		WR	WR	$P(R) = \frac{1}{2}$
				$P(W) = \frac{1}{2}$
		W	WRR	$P(R) = \frac{1}{3}$
				$P(W) = \frac{2}{3}$
		R	WWR	$P(R) = \frac{2}{3}$
				$P(W) = \frac{1}{3}$
	Which is the best arrangement?	H1: W and H2: WRR		

Activity 6 *Summarize*

TEACHER ACTION	TEACHER TALK	EXPECTED RESPONSE
Pass out Worksheet 6-2, Darts, Anyone? Illustrate the method of attacking these problems, which is to partition the area into equal squares. Put problem 1 on the board or the overhead.		
<table><tr><td colspan="2">A</td><td rowspan="3">A</td><td>B</td></tr><tr><td colspan="2">B</td><td>A</td></tr><tr><td colspan="2">A</td><td rowspan="2">B</td></tr><tr><td>B</td><td>A</td><td>B</td></tr></table>	What lines should I add to have equal areas?	Various answers.
Mark student responses on the grid.	One good way to approach these problems is to first make equal partitions horizontally and then vertically (or vice versa).	
A A A B B B A A A A A B B A B B	How many equal areas (squares) do we have?	16.
	What is the probability of A?	$P(A) = \frac{9}{16}$
	What is the probability of B?	$P(B) = \frac{7}{16}$
	Is this fair?	No.
	How can we make it fair?	Change one **A** square to a **B** square or let the **A** player get 7 points and the **B** player get 9 points.
Discuss the problems on Worksheet 6-2, giving correct solutions or having students give correct solutions. Let some students show their paths and the analysis for the maze in part II, or have students exchange papers and try to figure out each others' probabilities.	In problem 2 on Worksheet 6-2, when we make the horizontal lines needed and then the vertical lines needed, we see that the basic area into which we partition the board is smaller than *any* of the original areas.	If students have trouble weighting games in problems 3 and 4 on Worksheet 6-2, remind them that they want P(**X** points) for one player to equal P(**X** points) for the other(s). So in problem 4 we want to put numbers in □ and △ so that $\frac{7}{16} \times \square = \frac{9}{16} \times \triangle$.

TEACHER ACTION	TEACHER TALK	EXPECTED RESPONSE
Extra challenge.	Suppose you have RRR, WWW, and three hats to place them in. How would you arrange them to optimize the probability of drawing a red?	R / R / WW WR $P(R) = \frac{3}{4}$

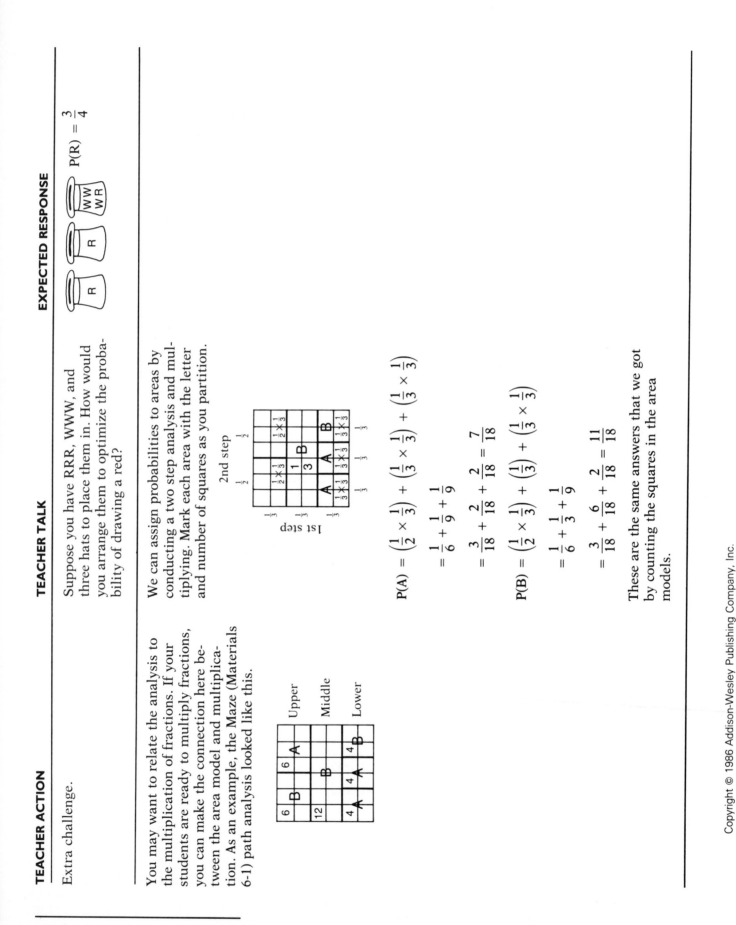

TEACHER ACTION

You may want to relate the analysis to the multiplication of fractions. If your students are ready to multiply fractions, you can make the connection here between the area model and multiplication. As an example, the Maze (Materials 6-1) path analysis looked like this.

6 B 6 A — Upper
12 B — Middle
4 A 4 A 4 B — Lower

TEACHER TALK

We can assign probabilities to areas by conducting a two step analysis and multiplying. Mark each area with the letter and number of squares as you partition.

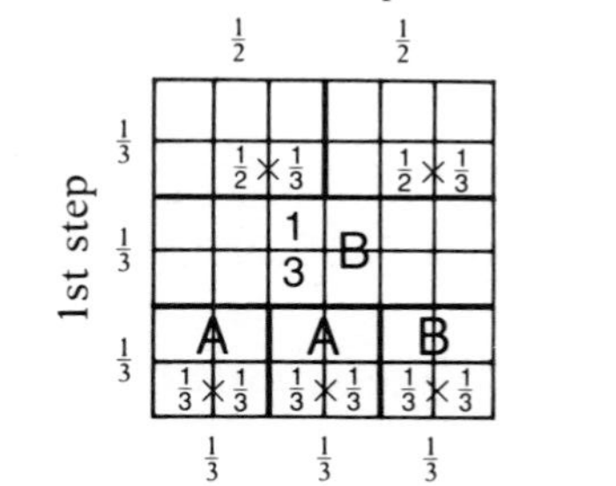

$$P(A) = \left(\frac{1}{2} \times \frac{1}{3}\right) + \left(\frac{1}{3} \times \frac{1}{3}\right) + \left(\frac{1}{3} \times \frac{1}{3}\right)$$

$$= \frac{1}{6} + \frac{1}{9} + \frac{1}{9}$$

$$= \frac{3}{18} + \frac{2}{18} + \frac{2}{18} = \frac{7}{18}$$

$$P(B) = \left(\frac{1}{2} \times \frac{1}{3}\right) + \left(\frac{1}{3}\right) + \left(\frac{1}{3} \times \frac{1}{3}\right)$$

$$= \frac{1}{6} + \frac{1}{3} + \frac{1}{9}$$

$$= \frac{3}{18} + \frac{6}{18} + \frac{2}{18} = \frac{11}{18}$$

These are the same answers that we got by counting the squares in the area models.

Materials 6-1

The Maze

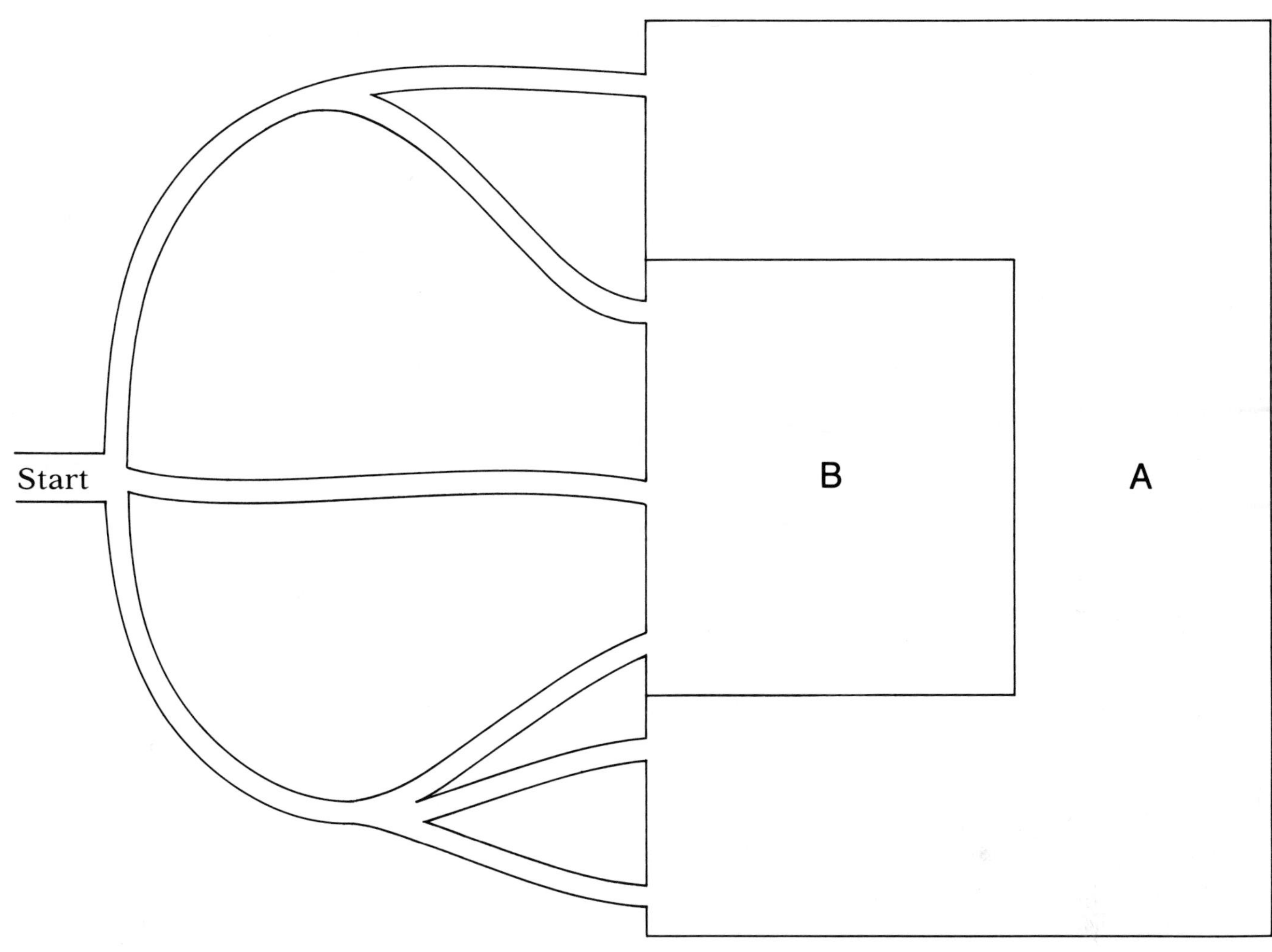

Materials 6-2

Another Maze

Start

B

A

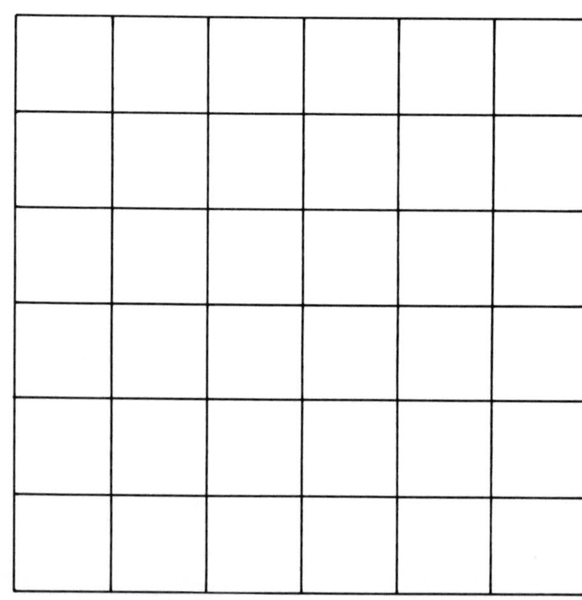

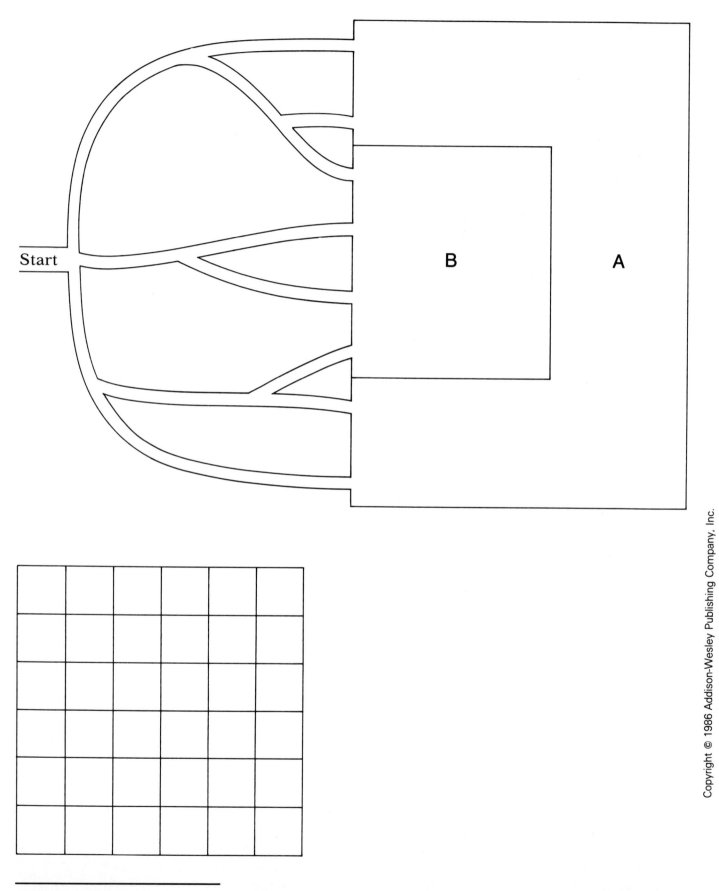

NAME ____________________

Which Is Best?

You are given two hats, two white marbles, and two red marbles. Which arrangement of the two white and two red marbles in the hats gives the best chance of drawing a white marble?

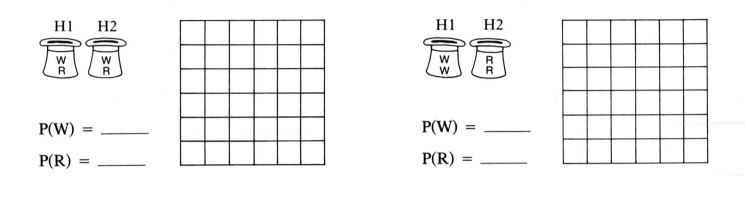

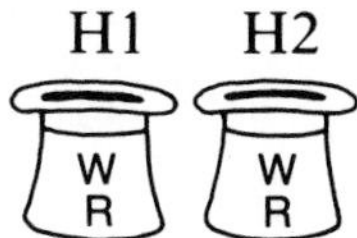

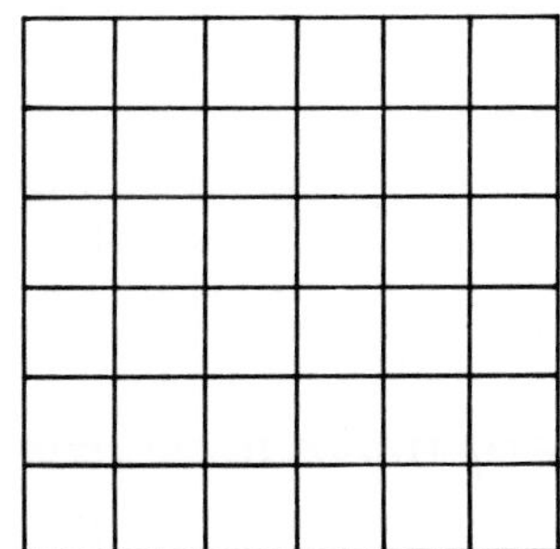

P(W) = ______

P(R) = ______

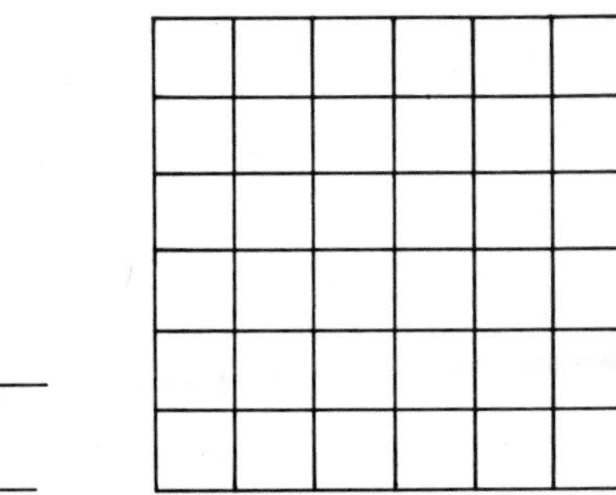

P(W) = ______

P(R) = ______

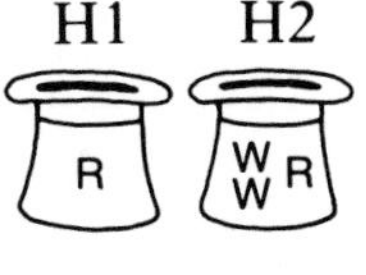

P(W) = ______

P(R) = ______

H1 H2

W

W R R

P(W) = ______

P(R) = ______

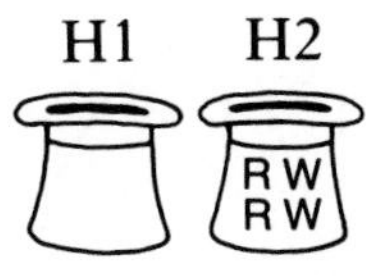

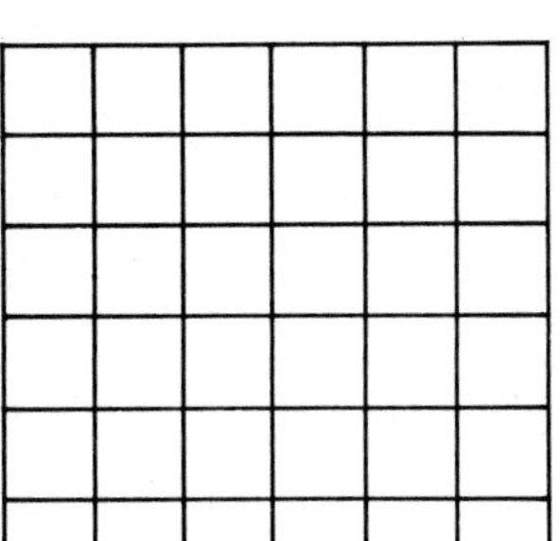

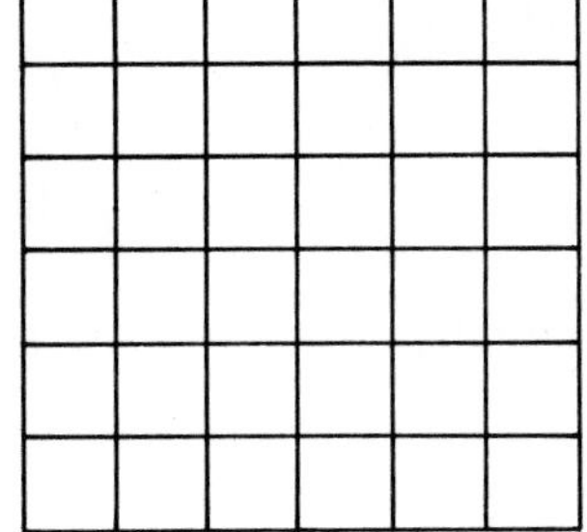

P(W) = ______

P(R) = ______

NAME ______________________

Darts, Anyone?

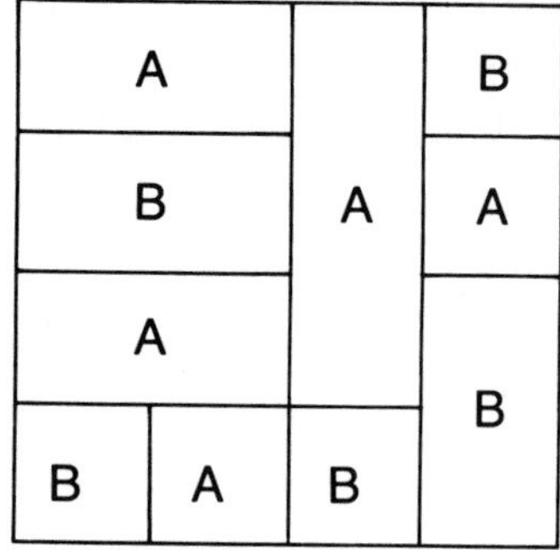

1. Pat and Erin are playing a game with the board shown at the right. A dart is thrown at random at the board. Pat scores a point if the dart lands in an area marked A. Erin scores a point if the dart lands in an area marked B. Is this a fair game?

   P(A) = ________ P(B) = ________

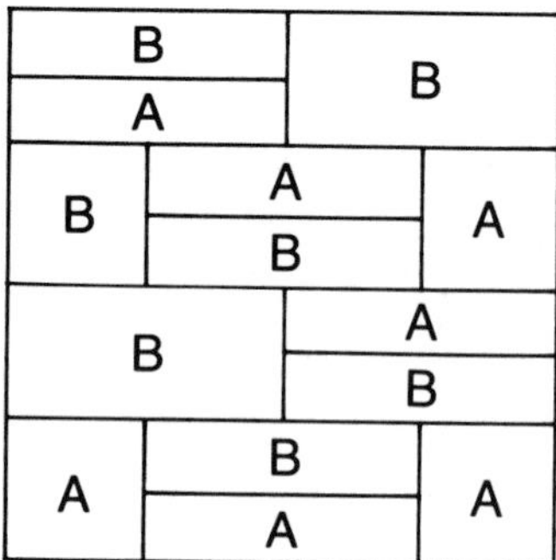

2. Find probabilities for this board. Would this board make a fair dart game?

   P(A) = ________ P(B) = ________

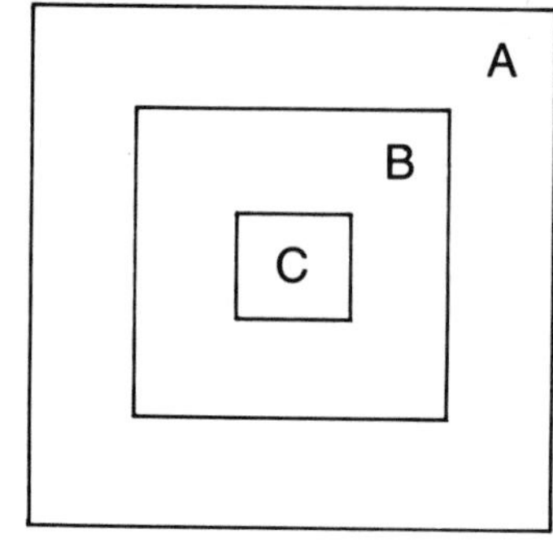

3. If a dart is thrown at random at this dart board, what is the probability that it will land in area A? What is the probability it will land in area B? What is the probability it will land in area C?

   P(A) = ________ P(B) = ________ P(C) = ________

   Scoring: If a dart landing in A scores one point, how many points should a dart landing in C score to make the two areas yield the same number of points over the long run? What should a dart in area B score?

   Points for C ________ Points for B ________

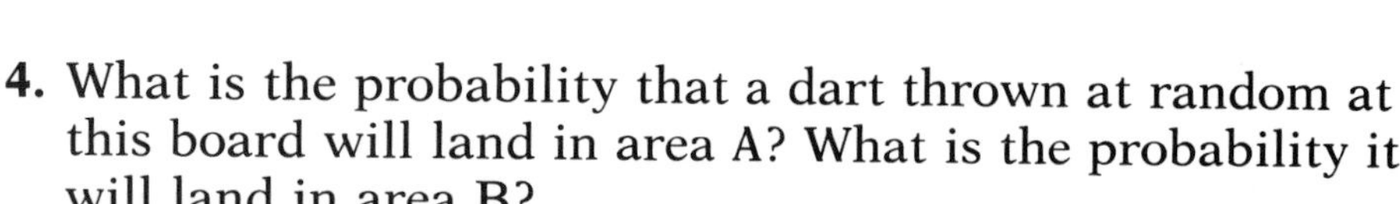

4. What is the probability that a dart thrown at random at this board will land in area A? What is the probability it will land in area B?

   P(A) = ________ P(B) = ________

   How would you assign points so that the game would be fair?

   Points for A ________ Points for B ________

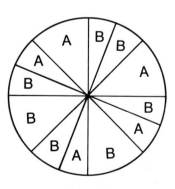

NAME ______________________

Darts, Anyone?

5. In the space below design a path for the story about Mr. Green and the students. Use the grid to analyze your path. Find the room in which the students should place the cookbook.

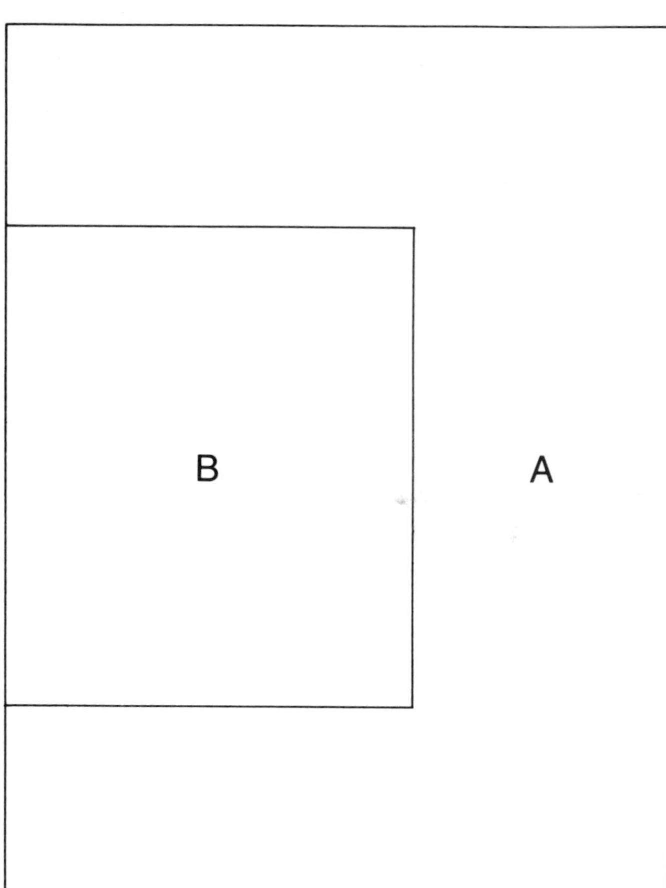

6. Jane used this grid to analyze a probability problem. What probabilities should be assigned to A, B, and C?

P(A) = ________ P(B) = ________ P(C) = ________

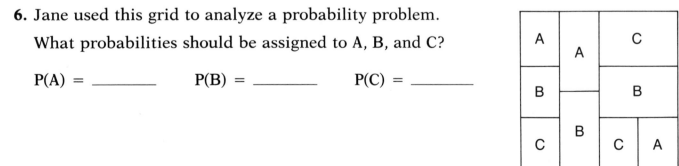

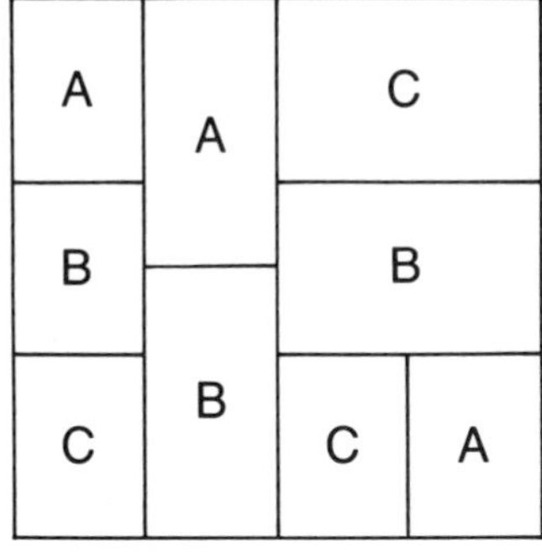

Activity 7

EXPECTED VALUE

OVERVIEW

In this activity we continue using the area model to analyze compound (dependent) events. The new idea is the average payoff over a very long run of trials. This is called the *expected value* of the situation. We have been informally dealing with this idea from the beginning. In our work on fair games we essentially made the expected value (payoff) for each player be the same to make the game fair.

A basketball game provides the story setting. Terry is a 60% ($\frac{60}{100}$) free-throw shooter and is in a one-and-one situation. (A team is in a one-and-one situation when the opposing team has collected a total of seven fouls; each time the team goes up for a free throw, they will get a second free throw if they make the first one.) We are interested in the following three questions:

1. On any given trip to the free throw line (trial) is Terry most likely to get 0 points, 1 point, or 2 points?
2. Over many trials, say 100, about how many total points would Terry expect to make?
3. Over the long run what is the average number of points per trip (or expected value)?

The questions are first answered experimentally and then theoretically. In the activity, the theoretical probabilities are figured as follows:

P(0 points) = probability of missing the first shot $= \frac{40}{100}$ or .40.

P(1 point) = probability of making the first shot *and* missing the second shot
$= \frac{60}{100} \times \frac{40}{100} = \frac{24}{100}$ or .24

P(2 points) = probability of making the first shot *and* making the second shot
$= \frac{60}{100} \times \frac{60}{100} = \frac{36}{100}$ or .36

In the simulation, the score 1 is *not* most likely to occur. This surprises students. Also, since the P(2 points) is very close to P(0 points), $\frac{36}{100} \approx \frac{40}{100}$, it is not easy to decide which of these two scores is most likely to occur. Thus, the experiment provides a real need to use a theoretical argument upon which to base our decisions.

Activity 7

Since we are working with dependent events, an area model is easy to use and understand. Some students may suggest using a tree diagram. This is awkward, because the events are not equally likely. If a tree is used, the branches would have to be weighted as follows:

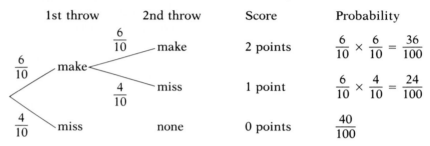

1st throw	2nd throw	Score	Probability
$\frac{6}{10}$ make	$\frac{6}{10}$ make	2 points	$\frac{6}{10} \times \frac{6}{10} = \frac{36}{100}$
	$\frac{4}{10}$ miss	1 point	$\frac{6}{10} \times \frac{4}{10} = \frac{24}{100}$
$\frac{4}{10}$ miss	none	0 points	$\frac{40}{100}$

The analysis for questions 2 and 3 is done in several steps:

In 100 trials, the number of times 0 points occur is
$P(0) \times 100 = \frac{40}{100} \times 100 = 40.$

In 100 trials, the number of times 1 point occurs is
$P(1) \times 100 = \frac{24}{100} \times 100 = 24.$

In 100 trials, the number of times 2 points occur is
$P(2) \times 100 = \frac{36}{100} \times 100 = 36.$

$$\text{Total points} = (40 \times 0 \text{ points}) + (24 \times 1 \text{ point}) + (36 \times 2 \text{ points}) = 96 \text{ points}$$

$$\text{Long Term Average} = \frac{\text{total points}}{\text{total trials}} = \frac{96 \text{ points}}{100 \text{ trials}} = .96 \text{ points per trial}$$

Any number of trials could be used and the theoretical result would be the same; it is convenient to multiply a decimal by 100.

Goals for students

1. Use probabilities to make predictions.
2. Express probability both as a fraction and as a decimal.
3. Calculate the expected value or long-term average.
4. Understand simulation by gathering data, organizing data, and analyzing data.
5. Practice using area models to analyze compound situations.
6. If appropriate, connect area models with multiplying fractions.

Materials

15 bobby pins or 15 bags with six red marbles and four white marbles each.

Worksheets

*7-1, Terry's Trials
*7-2, One-and-One Basketball Shots

Transparencies

Starred items should be made into transparencies.

EXPECTED VALUE

TEACHER ACTION	TEACHER TALK	EXPECTED RESPONSE
Explain.	Today we are going to look at a problem to do with basketball. How many of you have played basketball? Who can tell us what a one-and-one free throw situation is in a basketball game?	You get to take a shot from the free throw line and you get to take a second shot *if you ring the first one.*
Ask.	What are the possible points a basketball player may get in a one-and-one situation?	0 points, 1 point, and 2 points.
	Explain how each of these can happen.	0 points if the first shot is missed. 1 point if the first is made and the second missed. 2 points if both are made.
Tell a story.	Coach Mudd has kept a record of Terry's performance at the free throw line and has determined that Terry rings 60% of her shots.	
Ask.	Out of 100 trips to the line, about how many would you expect her to hit? How many would you expect her to miss?	60, 40
	How could we express the probability of her hitting a shot from the free throw line?	$\frac{60}{100}$ or .6 (or other equivalent expression in decimals or fractions)
	How could we express the probability of her missing a shot from the free throw line?	$\frac{40}{100}$ or .4, etc.
	We want to analyze what happens when Terry goes to the line in a one-and-one situation. We know what to expect when she takes a single shot, but in a one-and-one situation she might take two shots in a row. She might score 1 point, 2 points, or no points.	
Ask. Record the vote totals on the board.	Is Terry the most likely to score 1 point, 2 points, or 0 points?	Students will generally vote for 1 point.

Activity 7 *Launch*

TEACHER ACTION	TEACHER TALK	EXPECTED RESPONSE
	Let's simulate Terry's trips to the line in a one-and-one situation. This should give us an idea of what we could expect to happen.	
Display a transparency of Worksheet 7-1, Terry's Trials (spinner). Illustrate on the overhead. 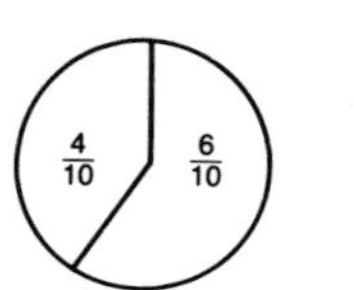	We can use a spinner with its area divided to represent the chances of hitting the shot, $\frac{6}{10}$, and the chances of missing the shot, $\frac{4}{10}$.	
Place a pen through a bobby pin at the center of the circle to use as a spinner.	Now, I'll spin the spinner. What does the result mean?	If the spinner stops in the $\frac{6}{10}$ area then Terry made the shot. If it stops in the $\frac{4}{10}$ area, she missed and gets 0 points.
Repeat spins until the spinner lands in both areas so that students have seen an example of each.		

TEACHER ACTION	TEACHER TALK	EXPECTED RESPONSE
Illustrate. First Spin / Second Spin First spin in $\frac{4}{10}$ area: 0 points First spin in $\frac{6}{10}$ area, second spin in $\frac{4}{10}$ area: 1 point First spin in $\frac{6}{10}$ area, second spin in $\frac{6}{10}$ area: 2 points	Now if she rings the first shot, what should we do?	Spin again.
	To summarize:	
	If the first spin is in the $\frac{4}{10}$ area, Terry gets 0 points.	
	If the first spin is in the $\frac{6}{10}$ area we spin again.	
	If the second spin is in the $\frac{4}{10}$ area Terry gets 1 point.	
	If the second spin is in the $\frac{6}{10}$ area Terry gets 2 points.	
Pair off class.	Now take turns and each of you simulate Terry at the free throw line for 20 trials.	
Ask.	What would be the maximum number of shots Terry could get in 20 trials?	40
	What would be the minimum number?	20
	So this means you will spin between 20 and 40 times to simulate Terry's trials.	
	Carefully record your results.	
Pass out Worksheet 7-1, Terry's Trials, and bobby pins.		

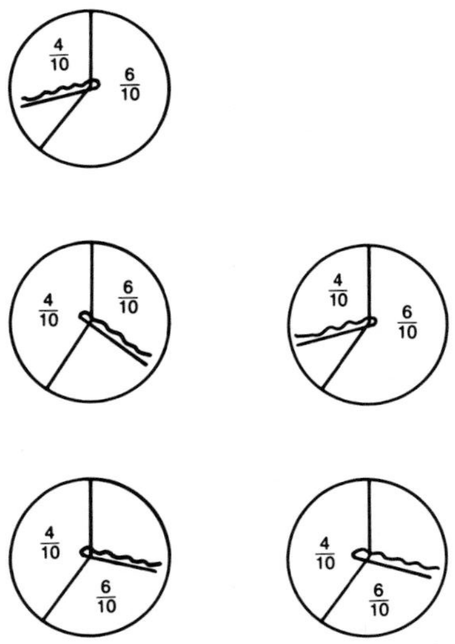

Activity 7 *Explore*

OBSERVATIONS	POSSIBLE RESPONSES
	Be sure to go around to the pairs of students and check to see that they are correctly gathering and recording their data. As an extra challenge, devise another way to simulate Terry at the free throw line. For instance, put six red marbles and four white marbles in a bag and draw at random.

Activity 7 *Summarize*

TEACHER ACTION	TEACHER TALK	EXPECTED RESPONSE
If three students are given a calculator and the responsibility of adding the 0s, 1s and 2s as they are collected, the summary can be made much more quickly.	Let's collect all the data for a whole class summary. Give me the number of times you got each result when I call on you. Be ready so that we can collect this quickly.	

Illustrate.

Class Data

Score / Groups	1	2	3	4	5	6	7	8	9	10	11	12	13	14	15	Totals	Probability	As a Decimal
0																		
1																		
2																		
															Total Number of Trials			

Now we can approximate the probability of Terry getting 0, 1, or 2 points by computing the experimental probabilities—the totals divided by the total trials, or $\frac{\text{totals}}{\text{total trials}}$.

TEACHER ACTION	TEACHER TALK	EXPECTED RESPONSE
Numbers are included as an example.		

Number of Points	Number of results
0	210
1	134
2	196
Number of Trials	540

Approximate probabilities for the example.

$\frac{210}{540} = .39$

$\frac{134}{540} = .25$

$\frac{196}{540} = .36$

Be sure to keep a record of the class data.

TEACHER ACTION	TEACHER TALK	EXPECTED RESPONSE
	Now, what do you think is the result most likely to happen—0 points, 1 point, or 2 points?	0 points or 2 points.
	Many of you voted for 1 point, but it looks like 1 point is the least likely result!	
	If we were going to tell someone what we thought the probability is that Terry would get 0, 1, or 2 points, should we use the group's data or the class data?	The class data because the more times we simulate the better the data.

TEACHER ACTION	TEACHER TALK	EXPECTED RESPONSE
Pass out Worksheet 7-2, One-and-One Basketball Shots.	Let's use an area model to analyze the problem. Then we'll compare the exact probabilities with our simulation and see how good it was.	
Display a transparency of Worksheet 7-2, One-and-One Basketball Shots.		
Illustrate. 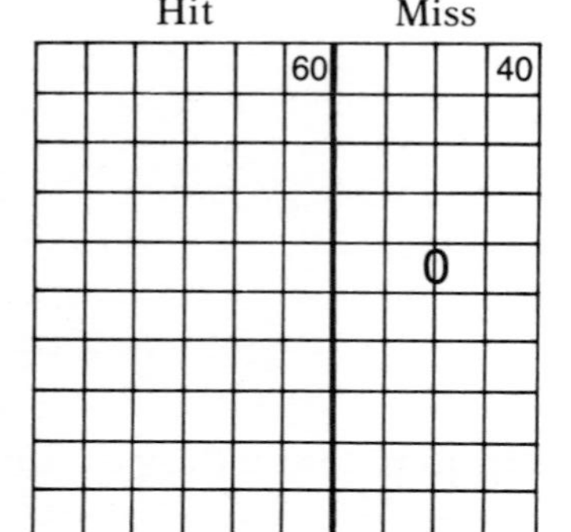	How should we partition the area to represent the first shot?	Draw a vertical line partitioning the area into $\frac{6}{10}$ and $\frac{4}{10}$.
	Do this on your worksheet as I illustrate at the overhead. This is problem 1.	
	We count six squares across the top row and make a vertical line partitioning the entire square into $\frac{6}{10}$ and $\frac{4}{10}$. This gives 60 squares in the Hit area and 40 squares in the Miss area.	
Illustrate. 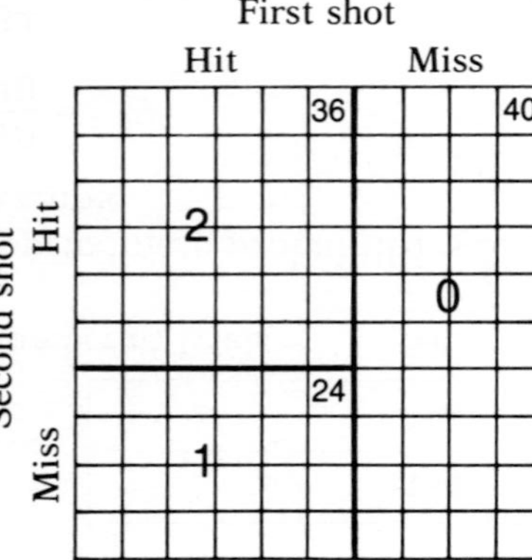	Now how can we partition the area for a hit the first time, to show the probabilities of hitting and missing the second shot?	Draw a horizontal line six squares down from the top.

TEACHER ACTION	TEACHER TALK	EXPECTED RESPONSE
You may want to have students multiply probabilities. If students are ready, you can again illustrate the connection by multiplying fractions or decimals.	Now how many of the small squares represent 0 points?	40
	How many represent 1 point?	24
	How many represent 2 points?	36
	How would we express these points as probabilities?	$\frac{40}{100}, \frac{24}{100}, \frac{36}{100}$ (or as decimals .40, .24, .36)

Outcomes for a one-and-one	Score	Probability
Miss	0	$P(0) = .4$ or $\frac{40}{100}$
Hit × Miss	1	$P(1) = .6 \times .4$ or $\frac{60}{100} \times \frac{40}{100}$
Hit × Hit	2	$P(2) = .6 \times .6$ or $\frac{60}{100} \times \frac{60}{100}$

These are the same as the numbers obtained by counting.

Compare these theoretical probabilities with the experimental probabilities. The two usually are quite close. It is usually easy to see that 1 is the least likely result. Since 0 and 2 have nearly equal probabilities, the experimental results may not show that we would expect 0 to occur a few more times than 2.

TEACHER ACTION	TEACHER TALK	EXPECTED RESPONSE
Illustrate.	Now let's look at the class results again. In the total number of trials, how many points did Terry score?	□
	How did we calculate this?	A score of 0 occurred □ times. A score of 1 occurred □ times. A score of 2 occurred □ times. or (0 × □) + (1 × □) + (2 × □) = □ points

Possible Scores	Number of times it occurred	Points scored
0	210	0
1	134	134
2	196	392
	540	526
	Total trials	Total points

The numbers in the chart above are only an illustration. Your class data will be different.

TEACHER ACTION	TEACHER TALK	EXPECTED RESPONSE
Ask.	Since we simulated Terry at the line in a one-and-one situation □ times, how many points did she *average* over the long run on a trip to the line?	[trials] / [total] points
	Can we change this to a decimal?	Yes.
	What is it equal to?	□ points.
	Good. That's an average of about 1 point per trip.	
	About how many points should 100 trips to the line yield in a one-and-one situation?	About 100 (a little less).

TEACHER ACTION	TEACHER TALK	EXPECTED RESPONSE
All these expected value problems can be done with younger students by looking at *100* trials (or any other convenient number you choose).	Now let's do the same thing using exact probabilities from the area model analysis. Let's use 100 trials.	
	In 100 trials how many 0s can we expect?	$100 \times \frac{40}{100} = 40$
	How many 1s?	$100 \times \frac{24}{100} = 24$
	How many 2s?	$100 \times \frac{36}{100} = 36$
	So how many points would we expect Terry to score in 100 trips?	$(0 \times 40) + (24 \times 1) + (2 \times 36) =$ 96 points.
	What is the average per trip?	$\frac{96}{100} = .96$, or nearly 1, as we saw from our experiment.
	This is *about* 1 point per trip!	
Tell.	The average number of points per trip is called the *expected value*. We usually compute the expected value over many trips (or trials) and think of it as a long-term average.	
	Use your grids to analyze shooters with percentages of 20%, 40%, and 80%.	
	Find the *expected value* (long-term average) for each player you analyze.	
Summarize Worksheet 7-2. Go over the procedure to be sure students understand. If you feel another example is needed, do the analysis for a 30%, 70%, or 90% shooter before letting the students do the worksheet.		
When the students have finished their analyses, go over the summary. Be sure students see how the most likely outcome changes and the long-term average grows.		

TEACHER ACTION	TEACHER TALK	EXPECTED RESPONSE

As an extra challenge, devise other ways to simulate each of the shooters. Try using marbles, dice, coins, or spinners.

Go back to the lottery in Activity 1 and find the exact probabilities for each person.

For 10-34 the probabilities would be

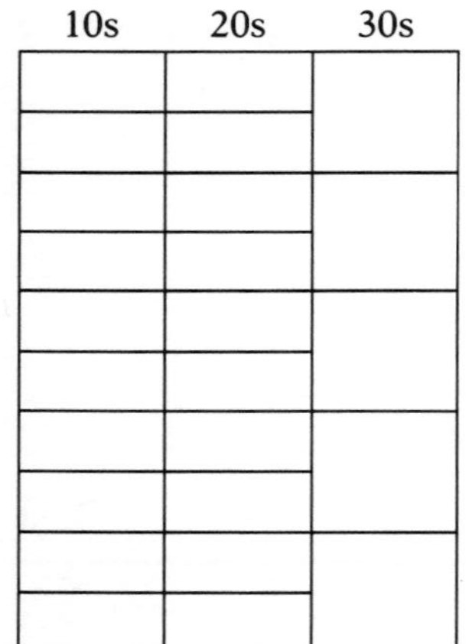

or $\frac{1}{3} \times \frac{1}{10} = \frac{1}{30}$ for the 10s

$\frac{1}{3} \times \frac{1}{10} = \frac{1}{30}$ for the 20s

and $\frac{1}{3} \times \frac{1}{5} = \frac{1}{15}$ for the 30s (or $\frac{2}{30}$)

NAME ____________________

Terry's Trials

Points	Frequency	Total	Approximate Probabilities
0			$\frac{\ }{20}$
1			$\frac{\ }{20}$
2			$\frac{\ }{20}$
	Number of Trials	20	

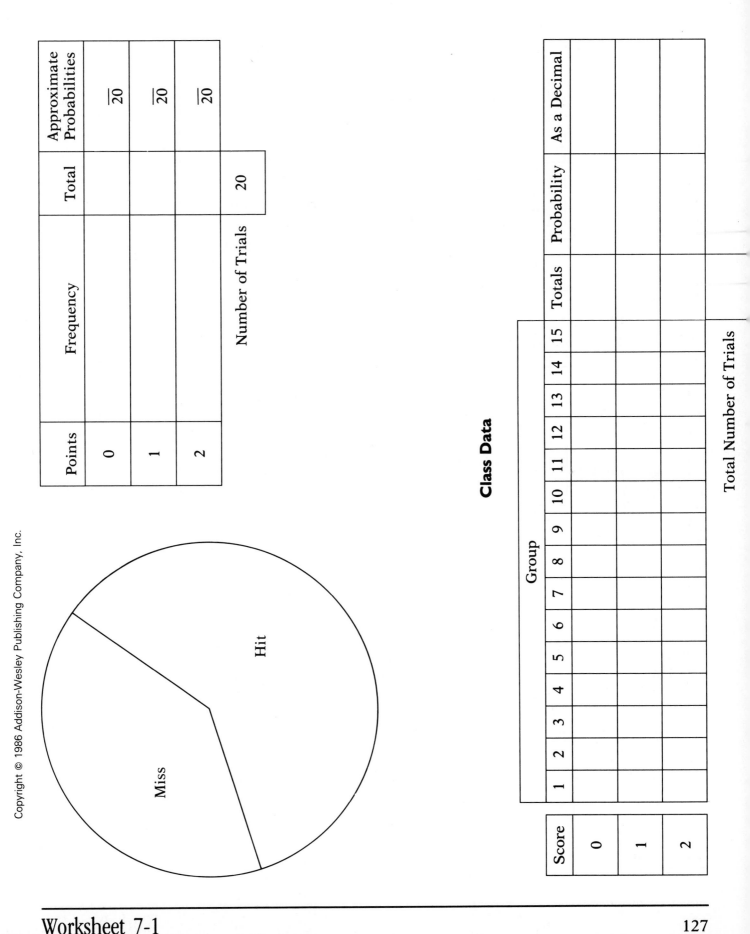

Miss

Hit

Class Data

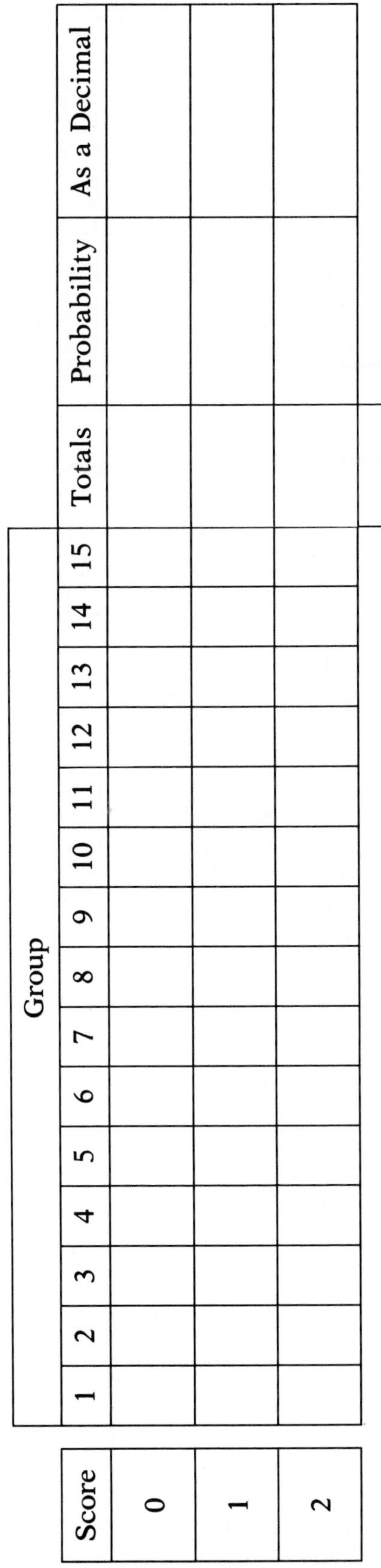

Score	Group 1	2	3	4	5	6	7	8	9	10	11	12	13	14	15	Totals	Probability	As a Decimal
0																		
1																		
2																		
															Total Number of Trials			

NAME ______________________

One-And-One Basketball Shots

60% Shooter (60% = $\frac{60}{100}$ or $\frac{6}{10}$)

P(0) = ______

P(1) = ______

P(2) = ______

Most likely outcome ______.

Average points per trip ______.

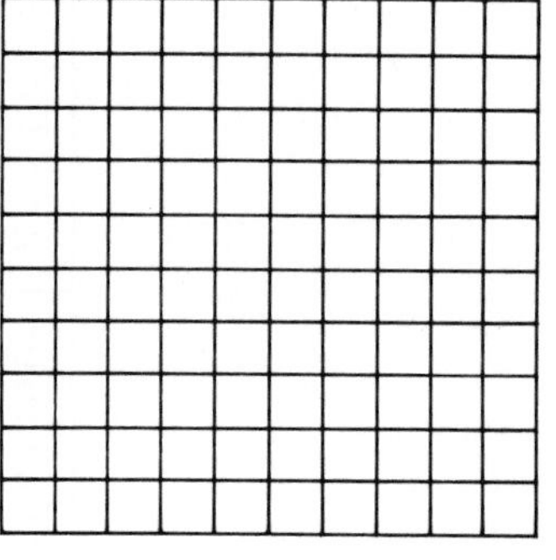

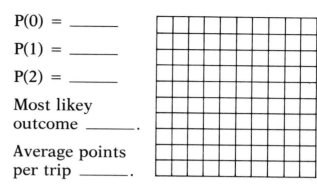

40% Shooter (40% = $\frac{40}{100}$ or $\frac{4}{10}$)

P(0) = ______

P(1) = ______

P(2) = ______

Most likey outcome ______.

Average points per trip ______.

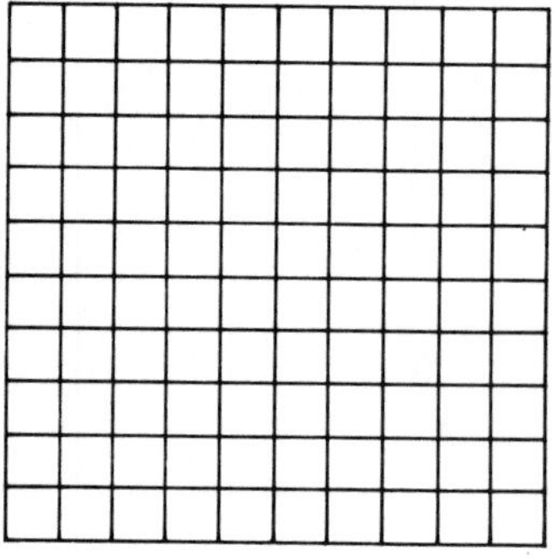

20% Shooter

P(0) = ______

P(1) = ______

P(2) = ______

Most likely outcome ______.

Average points per trip ______.

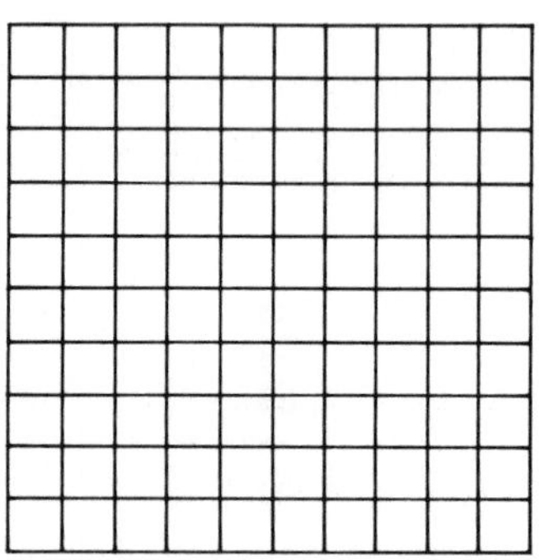

80% Shooter

P(0) = ______

P(1) = ______

P(2) = ______

Most likely outcome ______.

Average points per trip ______.

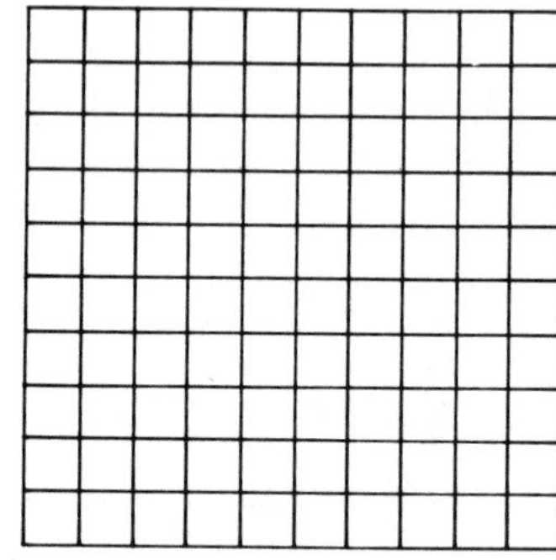

Summary

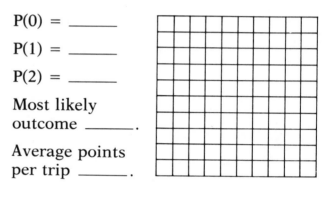

Shooter's Probability	Probability 0 points	1 point	2 points	Average points per trip
$\frac{2}{10}$				
$\frac{4}{10}$				
$\frac{6}{10}$				
$\frac{8}{10}$				

Activity 8 NEWSPAPER PAY

OVERVIEW

This is a summary activity for several themes that have previously been studied. The following problem is posed. A newspaper carrier is offered a choice by a customer of two pay plans: the usual \$5 a week, or the money received from drawing two bills out of a sack containing one \$10 bill and five \$1 bills. Two sums are possible: \$11 or \$2.

Students are given an opportunity to plan how to simulate the problem, to carry out the simulation, to analyze the problem theoretically, and to compare the results. The notions of expected value and fair games are combined in a more formal way, allowing students to review and reinforce both ideas. For example, the expected value (money) of drawing two bills from a sack is

$P(\$11) = \frac{5}{15} = \frac{1}{3}$ $\qquad$ $P(\$2) = \frac{10}{15} = \frac{2}{3}$

To find the expected value, we look at what happens in the long run. Since we have 3 in the probability denominators, let's look at 30 trials.

> The number of times we expect the newspaper carrier to get \$11 is $\frac{1}{3} \times 30$, or 10, times.
>
> She will get \$2 about $\frac{2}{3} \times 30$, or 20 times.
>
> Over the 30 weeks she will receive: $10 \times \$11 + 20 \times \$2 = \$150$.
>
> This is an average (or expected value) of $\frac{\$150}{30} = \$5$ per week.

So, if this pay plan is continued over many weeks this is a fair deal. The newspaper carrier should collect about the same under both plans.

The practice problems investigate some pay plans that are not fair over the long run. They also require reviewing many analyses that the students have done earlier, such as analyzing the outcome for tossing three coins or two dice.

Goals for students

1. Understand simulation by gathering, organizing, and analyzing data.
2. Devise a simulation plan.
3. Determine the expected value or long-term average.
4. Make organized lists of possible events.
5. Determine if games are fair or unfair.

Materials

Each group needs *one* of the following sets of items:

5 Ping Pong balls marked 1; 1 Ping Pong ball marked 10; 1 large sack.

Bobby pins for spinners and spinner bases.

6 stiff cards and 1 large sack.

One \$10 bill and five \$1 bills in play money & 1 large sack.

Worksheets

*8-1, The Newspaper Offer

8-2, Newspaper Pay

Transparencies

Starred item should be made into a transparency.

NEWSPAPER PAY

TEACHER ACTION	TEACHER TALK	EXPECTED RESPONSE
Tell a story.	Sue delivers newspapers for $5 a week per customer. One customer makes the following suggestion. Instead of my paying you $5 each week, let's make it more interesting. Each week I'll put five one-dollar bills and one ten-dollar bill in a paper sack. You'll reach in, without looking, and take two bills. You might only get $2, but you *might* get $11. How about it? Think it over tonight and give me your answer tomorrow.	
Ask. Record opinions.	Does this sound like a good deal to you? If you were Sue what would you do to help you make the decision?	Various answers. Simulate the drawing.
Place six Ping Pong balls in a sack. Have a volunteer draw two balls. Repeat five additional times. Each time, be sure to return the balls to the sack.	Let's simulate the drawing by using Ping Pong balls placed in a sack. One ball is marked 10 and five are marked 1.	
Record the number of $11 and $2 outcomes.	Did Sue come out ahead for the first six weeks?	($2 × □) + ($11 × □) = $□
Explain. Pass out Worksheet 8-1, The Newspaper Offer.	Six simulations may be too few to give us a true picture of Sue's chances. Let's simulate the drawing 30 times in each of the groups. The first thing you must do in your group is to plan a way to simulate the problem so that the data you gather will correctly represent Sue's possibilities. You have seen one way to do this using Ping Pong balls. You know that we have spinners, cards, marbles, discs, dice, coins, and various other items to use.	

TEACHER ACTION	TEACHER TALK	EXPECTED RESPONSE

Give the groups a few minutes to try to devise a simulation plan. If needed, give students a bag containing equipment that will allow one of the following methods, but put in too much equipment so that students still have to make some decisions.

The following are some reasonable ways to simulate the problem.

Use two spinners, one marked in six equal parts and one marked in five equal parts.

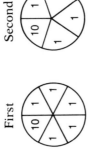

If the spin on the first spinner hits the 10, record an $11 outcome. If the spin on the first spinner hits a 1, spin again on the second and record $11 or $2 depending on what is hit.

Use six appropriately marked Ping Pong balls in a container. Six marbles or six discs could also be used.

Use six cards marked and shuffled (old playing cards can be marked and used).

Use paper money, one ten-dollar bill and five one-dollar bills in a sack (this requires *care* to see that the money is shuffled well each time).

(Be careful of dice. They do not allow the 5 options for the second throw.)

Activity 8 *Explore*

OBSERVATIONS	POSSIBLE RESPONSES
	Check each group to be sure they are using a correct simulation scheme. If a group finishes early, have them simulate in a different way and report on the comparative results. Did they feel one way was more random than the other, easier and faster to get good results, etc.? Ask students to describe ways to make sure that they are not influencing the outcomes. Elicit such responses as spin on a flat surface, etc.

Activity 8 *Summarize*

TEACHER ACTION	TEACHER TALK	EXPECTED RESPONSE
Ask.	Suppose Sue collected $5 every week for 30 weeks. How much is that?	$150.
Ask.	How many groups got more than $150? How many got less than $150? Did anybody get $150? What's the most any group got? What's the least any group got?	Various answers.

TEACHER ACTION	TEACHER TALK	EXPECTED RESPONSE
Display a transparency of Worksheet 8-1. Record each group's results in a table.	Let's record each group's data so that we can make a whole-class summary.	Add all the money and divide by the number of groups.
Example:	How would we find the *average* amount of money that each group totaled?	Approximately $150.
	Let's do the calculations. What do we get?	Approximately $5.
	If we divide this number by 30, we have the class average per trial. What is it?	Various answers.
	As a result of our class trials do you think this is a fair deal for Sue over the long run?	

Group	No. of $11	No. of $2	Total Money
1	9	21	$141
2			
3			
4			
5			
6			
⋮			
Totals			

Recording the class data on each student's sheet makes a permanent record that can be used to keep students who miss class up to date.

TEACHER ACTION	TEACHER TALK	EXPECTED RESPONSE
	We are going to analyze carefully what Sue can expect. Suppose these are the bills in the sack. We'll mark the ones 0_1, 0_2, 0_3, 0_4, 0_5, and the ten will be T.	
	Tell me one combination of two bills.	Various answers. (For a response "ten and one," ask "*which* one-dollar bill?")
Have students list combinations of bills worth $11 and worth $2.		

$T,0_1$	$0_1,0_2$	$0_2,0_3$	$0_3,0_4$	$0_4,0_5$
$T,0_2$	$0_1,0_3$	$0_2,0_4$	$0_3,0_5$	
$T,0_3$	$0_1,0_4$	$0_2,0_5$		
$T,0_4$	$0_1,0_5$			
$T,0_5$				

TEACHER ACTION	TEACHER TALK	EXPECTED RESPONSE
Some students may suggest using a tree diagram. This will give every outcome in both orders, such as $T0_1$ and 0_1T. The probabilities remain the same.		
Ask.	How many combinations are worth $11?	Five
	How many combinations are worth $2?	Ten
	What fraction (probability) of the ways is worth $11?	$P(\$11) = \frac{5}{15} = \frac{1}{3}$
	What fraction (probability) is worth $2?	$P(\$2) = \frac{10}{15} = \frac{2}{3}$
	One-third of the time, Sue expects $11.	
	Two-thirds of the time, Sue expects $2.	
Ask.	What would we expect the long-term average to be?	Various answers.
	Is this the same as the *expected value* of each draw?	Yes.
	In 30 draws, how many times will Sue expect to get $11? How many times will she expect to get $2?	Ten times 20 times
	How much money would this total? $\$11 \times 10 + \$2 \times 20 = \square$	$150
	Divide by 30 to get the average per draw. What is the average?	$5
Ask.	Is this a fair deal over the long run?	YES!
	Would you take the chance?	Various answers.
Pass out Worksheet 8-2, Newspaper Pay.	Here are some other situations for you to analyze. Decide which ones are fair.	
Do problems 1, 3, and 5 in class to make sure everyone has the correct procedures and understandings.		

NAME ____________________

The Newspaper Offer

1. Describe how you will conduct the experiment. What are you using to represent the money? How are you drawing out the money? Is the way you are collecting the money random?

Record your data.

Mark a tally in this box when Sue gets \$11.	Mark a tally in this box when Sue gets \$2.
Money collected: Total × \$11 = ______	Money collected: Total × \$2 = ______

Total number of trials = ______

Total money collected = ______

Long term average = $\frac{\text{Total money collected}}{\text{Total number of trials}}$ = ______

2. Class Data:

11s															
2s															

Total 11s = ______

Total 2s = ______

Total trials = ______

Total money collected = ______ × \$11 + ______ × \$2 = ______

Long term average = $\frac{\text{Total collected}}{\text{Total trials}}$ = ______

NAME

Newspaper Pay

In each of the following situations, the customer should pay $5 per week for newspapers. Sue, the paper carrier, has to decide which of the schemes of chance would give her a fair deal over the long run. In each case, decide what Sue should do—accept or reject the proposal.

1. The customer will place a five-dollar bill and 3 one-dollar bills in a bag. Sue will draw out two bills.

2. The customer will place a five-dollar bill and 2 one-dollar bills in a bag. Sue will draw out two bills.

3. Sue will toss three coins. If two or more land heads, Sue gets $9. Otherwise, she gets $1.

4. Sue will toss three coins. If all land the same, all heads or all tails, Sue gets $15. Otherwise, she gets $1.

5. Sue rolls a pair of dice. If the sum is exactly 7, Sue gets $20. Otherwise she gets $2.

6. Sue will roll a pair of dice. If the sum is at most 4, Sue will get $20. What should she get otherwise to make the payoff fair in the long run?

Activity 9

SMITHVILLE FAMILIES

OVERVIEW

Many interesting probability situations are of the type where there are exactly two possible responses: yes or no, boy or girl, true or false, heads or tails, etc. These are called *binomial* probabilities. (The term binomial is formally defined for students in Activity 10.) In this activity the peculiar families of Smithville, who all have exactly five children, are studied. The students are asked to generate some examples of possible Smith families and then to complete the list to include all possible Smith families. This results in a list of all possible ways to arrange five children according to numbers of boys and girls (bbggg, bgbgg, ggggg, etc.).

After the list for Smithville is complete, many complicated probability questions can be asked and answered easily by using the data from the list. For example, the probability that a family of 5 children will have *at most* 2 boys is satisfied by 0, 1, or 2 boys. The equation $\frac{1 + 5 + 10}{32}$ gives the correct solution.

An application problem involving George's chances of escape from Warwick Castle is posed, simulated, and finally analyzed. George's dilemma turns out to have exactly the same possibilities as the Smithville families. This gives the students a chance to see two problems that look different but have the same basic mathematical structure.

Goals for students

1. Make organized lists of the possible events.
2. Perform an experiment; compare graphically the results of experimental and theoretical analysis.
3. Demonstrate that a larger number of trials will give results that more clearly approach the theoretical probabilities.
4. Apply results of one situation to solve binomial application problem.

Materials

Map of your state (optional).

One coin for every pair of students.

*Summary of Smithville families (Materials 9-1; optional)

Worksheets

*9-1, Smithville Families

*9-2, Castle Warwick to Castle Howard

9-3, Record Sheet

Transparencies

Starred items should be made into transparencies.

SMITHVILLE FAMILIES

TEACHER ACTION	TEACHER TALK	EXPECTED RESPONSE
Select some small town in your state (or use Smithville) and show students where it is on the map.	There is a small town in our state named Smithville. Has anyone ever been there?	
Tell a story.	In Smithville, every family is named Smith, and every family has exactly 5 children! The parents in Smithville use only the following names for their children. 1. Bob Gina 2. Bill Gloria 3. Ben Ginny 4. Bud Gigi 5. Brad Gwen The names are assigned in this way. If the first child is a boy, he is named Bob; if a girl, she is named Gina. If the second child is a boy, he is named Bill; if a girl, she is named Gloria, and so on.	
Demonstrate. Flip a coin five times. H = Boy, T = Girl.	Let's look at an example of what a Smith family could be.	
Record the names on the board.	Let's use a coin to generate one Smith family together. Suppose you flipped T, T, H, T, H. The family we generated is 1. Gina 2. Gloria 3. Ben 3 girls, 2 boys 4. Gigi 5. Brad	
	If you are the fourth child in a Smithville family and you are a girl, what would your name be?	Gigi

TEACHER ACTION	TEACHER TALK	EXPECTED RESPONSE
If a student in your class is one of five children, ask for the sexes and order of birth and illustrate the names that would have been given to the family if they lived in Smithville.		
Ask. Record responses on the board.	We have seen a couple of different ways to name a Smith family's five children. How many distinct ways do you think there are to name the five children in a Smith family?	Various answers.
Direct. Pass out Worksheet 9-1, Smithville Families.	Let's gather some data. Working in pairs, generate seven Smith families and list them on your sheet.	
Discuss possible methods for simulating a family. Let each pair pick their own device.	How can we generate a Smith family? Choose an experimental device.	Dice Spinner Coin Chips Marbles Blocks Ping Pong balls

Activity 9 *Explore*

OBSERVATIONS	POSSIBLE RESPONSES
	Make sure each pair is randomly generating their families.
	Make sure they are listing the names in the correct order.

Activity 9 *Summarize*

TEACHER ACTION	TEACHER TALK	EXPECTED RESPONSE
Ask.	Let's organize the data you have gathered. Did anyone get the same family more than once?	Several teams will probably say yes.
Ask.	Did anyone have an all-girl family?	Several teams will probably say yes.
Ask a second team. Establish that all-girl families are alike.	What were their names?	
	How can I record an all-girl family without having to list all of the names?	G G G G G
Show students how to list families.	To whom does the third G refer?	Ginny
Ask.	How many different all-boy families can we have?	Only one. B B B B B

TEACHER ACTION	TEACHER TALK	EXPECTED RESPONSE
Ask.	Did anyone find a family with four girls and only one boy?	Several teams will probably say yes.
Ask one group at a time to list families with four girls and one boy.	What were their names?	The students will probably name all five different families with 4G, 1B. If they do not find all from their generated data, ask them to list any others that are possible. G G G G B G G G B G G G B G G G B G G G B G G G G
Ask.	How many families with four boys and only one girl?	Several teams will probably say yes. List the families and elicit any that are omitted. Some students will observe that this is the same as four girls and one boy—just interchange the Bs and Gs. B B B B G B B B G B B B G B B B G B B B G B B B B

TEACHER ACTION	TEACHER TALK	EXPECTED RESPONSE
Ask.		There will be many.
Here there are likely to be several possibilities that are not among the generated families. Encourage the students to organize their search for the missing ones by *systematically* listing the possibilities.	Who had a family with three girls and two boys? List them.	
For example, write down all the possibilities if the first child is a boy (4), if the first is a girl and second a boy (3), and finally, if the first two are girls (3).	Can we find a systematic way to list all the possibilities?	
Get students to recognize that to get two girls and three boys we can just interchange the Bs and Gs in the three girls and two boys column.	How about families with three boys and two girls?	

3 Girls, 2 Boys	2 Girls, 3 Boys
B B G G G	G G B B B
B G B G G	G B G B B
B G G B G	G B B G B
B G G G B	G B B B G
G B B G G	B G G B B
G B G B G	B G B G B
G B G G B	B G B B G
G G B B G	B B G G B
G G B G B	B B G B G
G G G B B	B B B G G

The final display should contain all the possibilities to be organized like this:

5 Girls, 0 Boys	4 Girls, 1 Boy	3 Girls, 2 Boys	2 Girls, 3 Boys	1 Girl, 4 Boys	0 Girls, 5 Boys
1	5	10	10	5	1
G G G G G	G G G G B	G G G B B	G G B B B	G B B B B	B B B B B
	G G G B G	G G B G B	G B G B B	B G B B B	
	G G B G G	G B G G B	G B B G B	B B G B B	
	G B G G G	B G G G B	G B B B G	B B B G B	
	B G G G G	G G B B G	B G G B B	B B B B G	
		G B G B G	B G B G B		
		B G G B G	B G B B G		
		G B B G G	B B G G B		
		B G B G G	B B G B G		
		B B G G G	B B B G G		

You may provide students with the Summary of Smithville Families (Materials 9-1), or have them make their own summary.

TEACHER ACTION	TEACHER TALK	EXPECTED RESPONSE
Conclude.	How many possible Smith families are there?	32 possible families in the pattern: 5G 1, 4G1B 5, 3G2B 10, 2G3B 10, 1G4B 5, 5B 1
You may wish to have students compare experimental and theoretical probabilities of families.	Let's look at the families from our experiment and see how close the experiment matches the theory. Label each of your families with the number of girls in that family.	
Collect and display data. The responses are based on an example of 44 trials to demonstrate the tallying method.	How many families were 5-girl families? How many families were 4-girl families? How many families were 3-girl families? How many families were 2-girl families? How many families were 1-girl families? How many families were 0-girl families?	(see tally below)

5G	4G1B	3G2B	2G3B	1G4B	5B
1	5	10	10	5	1

			X				
			X	X			
			X	X			
			X	X			
			X	X			
			X	X	X		
			X	X	X		
		X	X	X	X		
		X	X	X	X		
		X	X	X	X		
		X	X	X	X	X	
	X	X	X	X	X	X	
	X	X	X	X	X	X	
Number of Girls	5	4	3	2	1	0	
Total	2	6	13	12	8	3	= 44
Probabilities	$\frac{2}{44}$	$\frac{6}{44}$	$\frac{13}{44}$	$\frac{12}{44}$	$\frac{8}{44}$	$\frac{3}{44}$	

TEACHER ACTION	TEACHER TALK	EXPECTED RESPONSE
If your students have not done Computer Activity III, review with them how to convert a fraction into a decimal (or percent).	To compare our experiment with our analysis we need to convert the fractions showing the probabilities to decimals (or percents).	Experimental: $\frac{2}{44}$ $\frac{6}{44}$ $\frac{13}{44}$ $\frac{12}{44}$ $\frac{8}{44}$ $\frac{3}{44}$; Total $\frac{44}{44}$ % 4.5 13.6 29.5 27.3 18.2 6.8 100% Theoretical: $\frac{1}{32}$ $\frac{5}{32}$ $\frac{10}{32}$ $\frac{10}{32}$ $\frac{5}{32}$ $\frac{1}{32}$; Total $\frac{32}{32}$ % 3.1 15.6 31.2 31.2 15.6 3.1 100%
	How could we improve our experimental results?	Be sure we flip our coin randomly, collect more data, etc.
Refer to the list of theoretical outcomes on the board or on the Summary of Smithville Families (Materials 9-1).	Now let's answer some probability questions using our analytical data.	
Ask.	What is the probability that a family of 5 children will have 3 boys *and* 2 girls?	$\frac{10}{32}$
	What is the probability that a family of 5 children will have exactly 4 boys and 1 girl *or* 4 girls and 1 boy?	$\frac{5+5}{32} = \frac{10}{32}$
	What is the probability that a family of 5 children will have *at most* 2 boys? (This is satisfied by 2, 1, *or* 0 boys.)	$\frac{1+5+10}{32} = \frac{16}{32}$
	What is the probability that a family of 5 children will have *at least* 4 girls? (This is satisfied by 4 or 5 girls.)	$\frac{5+1}{32} = \frac{6}{32}$
Encourage students to make up some questions about the Smithville families. Let the class answer them.	What is the probability of the first child being a girl?	$\frac{1}{2}$; some students will count from the list to get $\frac{16}{32}$. Show them that this is not necessary. For any given child being a boy, the probability is $\frac{1}{2}$.

Activity 9 *Launch*

TEACHER ACTION	TEACHER TALK	EXPECTED RESPONSE
Tell the story of George.		
Pass out Worksheet 9-2, Castle Warwick to Castle Howard, and Worksheet 9-3, Record Sheet.		
Simulate the problem once as a class. Use a coin, a spinner, a die (odd/even), or another 50/50 device. Show how to tell whether there is an escape route.	Now each group should simulate the canal problem 20 times, recording your results on the recording sheet.	
For example, O means open, C means closed. OOCOC means O O C O C. ↑ ↑ ↑ ↑ ↑ gate 1 2 3 4 5 George can escape by using gates 1 and 4.	Consider this example OOCOC. Can George escape? Remember: George can search around and find any open route. The question asked is "Is a route open at a given time?"	Yes, by using gates 1 and 4. If students answer incorrectly they may be confusing this problem with the maze problem. Remind them that the question being asked is "Does an open route exist for a particular state of the gates?" *Not* "Does George *choose* an open route?"

Activity 9 *Explore*

OBSERVATIONS	POSSIBLE RESPONSES
One good way to simulate this problem is to use groups of six, one to record and five to play the role of the cranky gatekeepers. The five should flip simultaneously to simulate the real situation.	Make sure students are recording and interpreting the results correctly.

TEACHER ACTION	TEACHER TALK	EXPECTED RESPONSE
When the class has gathered its data, summarize the results. Find the class probabilities. P(Open Route) should be close to $\frac{19}{32}$.	When I call on your group, give me the total number of yeses that you got and the total number of nos. These should add up to 20.	
Ask.	Let's analyze the canal problem theoretically.	
	How many different arrangements of open-closed could we have for the five gates?	Various answers.
Ask.	Is the canal problem like any problem we have done before? Which one?	Yes; the Smithville problem.
	How many different arrangements did we find for Smithville families?	32
For more advanced students you can use the Smithville family. Let G = open and B = closed. For others write out the analysis using Os and Cs as follows:	Analyze each of the 32 outcomes to see if there is a path from A to B. From this analysis find the probability of George's escape.	

Analysis of George's problem

O = open　　C = closed
Y = yes there is a way to escape
N = no there is no escape

$$P(Y) = \frac{19}{32} = .59375$$

		OOCCC N	OOOCC Y		
		OCOCC Y	OOCOC Y		
		COOCC Y	OOCCO N		
		OCCOC Y	OCOOC Y		
		COCOC N	OCOCO Y		
	OCCCC N	CCOOC N	OCCOO Y	OOOOC Y	
	COCCC N	OCCCO N	COOOC Y	OOOCO Y	
	CCOCC N	COCCO N	COOCO Y	OOCOO Y	
	CCCOC N	CCOCO N	COCOO Y	OCOOO Y	
CCCCC N	CCCCO N	CCCOO Y	CCOOO Y	COOOO Y	OOOOO Y
12345 Gates	12345 Gates	12345 Gates	12345 Gates	12345 Gates	12345 Gates

Summary of Smithville Families

5 Girls 1	4 Girls 5	3 Girls 10	2 Girls 10	1 Girl 5	0 Girls 1
GGGGG	GGGGB	GGGBB	GGBBB	GBBBB	BBBBB
	GGGBG	GGBGB	GBGBB	BGBBB	
	GGBGG	GBGGB	GBBGB	BBGBB	
	GBGGG	BGGGB	GBBBG	BBBGB	
	BGGGG	GGBBG	BGGBB	BBBBG	
		GBGBG	BGBGB		
		BGGBG	BGBBG		
		GBBGG	BBGGB		
		BGBGG	BBGBG		
		BBGGG	BBBGG		

NAME ______________

Smithville Families

Names	
1. BOB GINA 2. BILL GLORIA 3. BEN GINNY 4. BUD GIGI 5. BRAD GWEN	1. 2. 3. 4. 5.
1. 2. 3. 4. 5.	1. 2. 3. 4. 5.
1. 2. 3. 4. 5.	1. 2. 3. 4. 5.
1. 2. 3. 4. 5.	1. 2. 3. 4. 5.

Guess how many different sets of names are possible for Smithville families.

Record your guess here. ______

NAME ____________________

Castle Warwick To Castle Howard

Our hero George is trapped at Castle Warwick. The only escape is to reach Castle Howard through a system of canals. The problem is that the system of canals has five gatehouses, each run by a cranky gatekeeper who shows up for work about half the time. So the probability that a gate is open on a given day is one half. The arrows show the way the water flows through the canals.

What is the probability that a water route from Castle Warwick to Castle Howard is open so that George can escape on the day chosen? (We assume that our hero will find it if a route is open.)

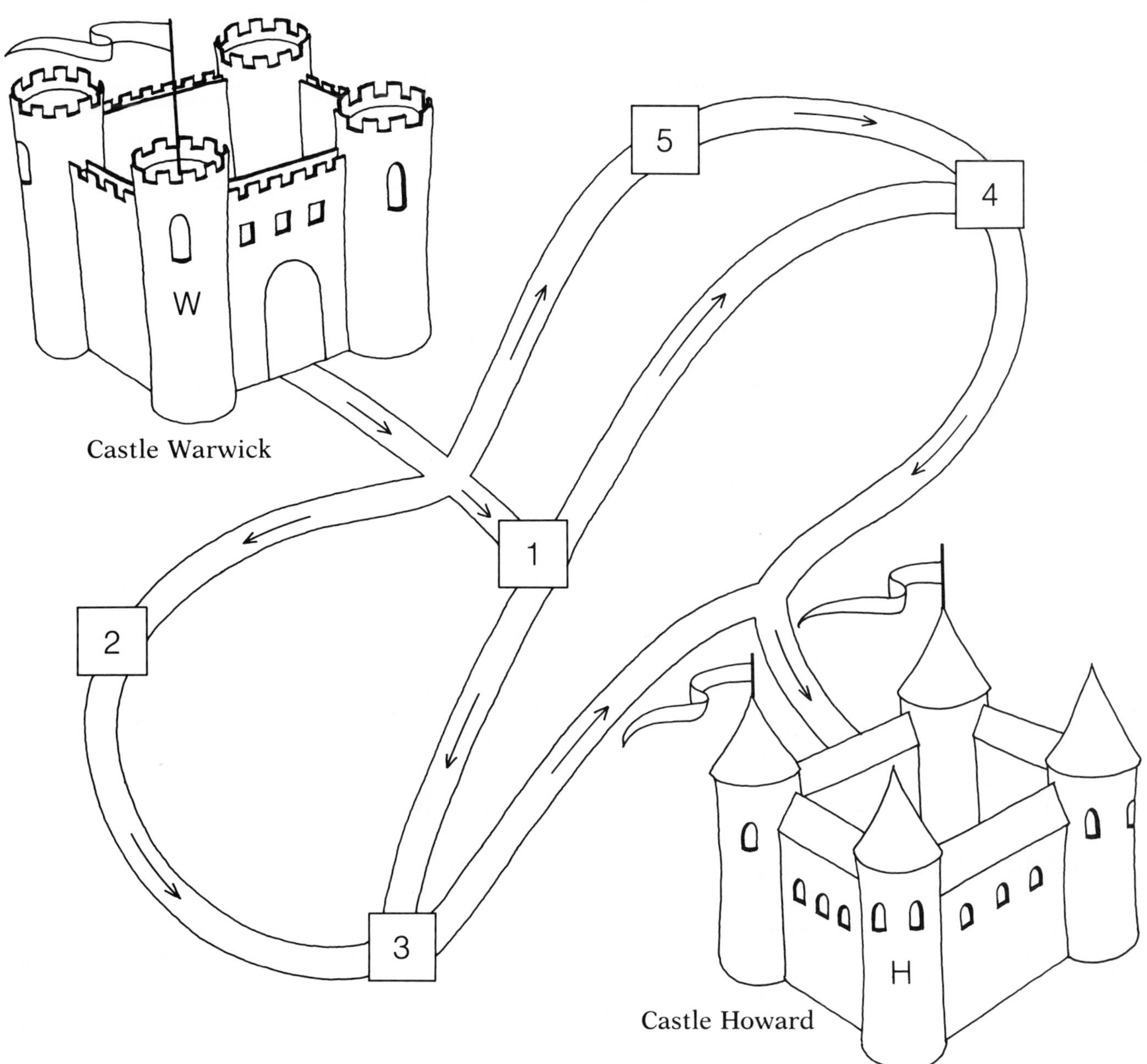

NAME ______________________

Record Sheet

Trials	Gates					Path Open/Closed
	1	2	3	4	5	
1						
2						
3						
4						
5						
6						
7						
8						
9						
10						
11						
12						
13						
14						
15						
16						
17						
18						
19						
20						

Total Yes = ________ Total No = ________

Probability of Yes is ________ Probability of No is ________

Class Data																	Totals	Probability	Decimal
Yes's																			
No's																			

Activity 10

PASCAL'S TRIANGLE

OVERVIEW

This activity continues the work done in Activity 9. Two additional problems that can be analyzed using the Smithville data are posed, the World Series problem and the Five-Item True-False Test problem. Finally, data is collected from binomial examples analyzed earlier in the unit to fill in the first few rows of Pascal's Triangle.

In the World Series between the evenly matched Giraffes and Bears, the Giraffes have won the first two games. This results in two questions: What is the probability the Giraffes will win the series? What is the probability the series ends in 4, 5, 6, or 7 games? The probability of the Giraffes winning is $\frac{26}{32}$, and the probabilities that the game ends in 4, 5, 6, or 7 are all the same—$\frac{8}{32}$ or $\frac{1}{4}$.

In the second activity, students are asked to take a Five-Item True-False Test. The teacher pretends to lose the questions but tells the students to fill in the answers anyway. The question here is: What is the probability that a student will have a perfect paper by guessing. The probability is $\frac{1}{32}$.

Pascal's Triangle is used to summarize binomial probabilities and to answer new questions on binomial situations. The triangle of numbers is named after the 17th century mathematician Blaise Pascal, because he was the first to apply this special array of numbers to probability. However, this triangular array of numbers was in existence long before Pascal applied it to probabilities. It was found in a 14th century book by a Chinese mathematician and was referred to by the 12th century poet Omar Khayyám, who was also a mathematician.

The rows of Pascal's Triangle could be applied to the flipping of coins or to the number of children in a family.

Pascal's Triangle	Coins	Children
1 1	flipping one coin	1-child family
1 2 1	flipping two coins	2-child family
1 3 3 1	flipping three coins	3-child family
1 4 6 4 1	flipping four coins	4-child family
1 5 10 10 5 1	flipping five coins	5-child family

From this start, patterns are observed that help us to generate additional rows of the triangle. Finally, probability problems are posed, which can be solved by taking data from the appropriate row of the triangle.

Goals for students

1. Classify situations as binomial events.
2. Develop Pascal's Triangle.
3. Use Pascal's Triangle to solve application problems involving binomial probability situations.
4. Practice finding expected values (long-term averages).

Activity 10

Materials

Coins for flipping.
*Summary of Smithville Families (Materials 9-1).

Worksheets

10-1, Pascal's Triangle
10-2, Pascal's Triangle Follow-Up

Transparencies

Starred item should be made into a transparency.

PASCAL'S TRIANGLE

TEACHER ACTION	TEACHER TALK	EXPECTED RESPONSE
The results of the Smithville families should still be on the board without any attention being called to them at this stage.		
Give the setting for the problem.	Every year the best baseball team from the American League plays the best baseball team from the National League in the World Series of Professional Baseball. The Series is a best of seven series, which means that the first team to win four games wins the series.	
	Let's pretend that two evenly matched teams, the Bears and the Giraffes, are playing in the World Series. That is, each team is equally likely to win each game. Two games have been played, and the Giraffes have won both games.	
	What do you think the probability is that the Giraffes will win the series?	Various answers.
	What do you think the probability is that the Bears will win the series?	Various answers.
Ask.	If we were going to simulate the series, what are some methods that we could use?	Flipping a coin (heads for Bears, tails for Giraffes); using a spinner, etc. G | B
Ask.	How many possible games are left in the series?	5 games.
	The next games might be BGGGB, B for Bears and G for Giraffes.	
	Who would win?	The Giraffes.
	Does this sound like anything we have done before? What?	Yes, the Smith families.

TEACHER ACTION	TEACHER TALK	EXPECTED RESPONSE
Direct.	Good. We can analyze this situation using our list for the Smith families. We know that our list includes every possible arrangement of Bs and Gs so it must contain all possible series. Let's go through the list and determine who will win each possible series. At the same time let's put down the number of games played to determine a winner.	
Go through the list with the class and place a G or B after each series to indicate the winner and length of series. Example: GBGGG (g-5)—Giraffes win in five games.		

GGGGG (g-4)	**GGGGB (g-4)**	**GGGBB (g-4)**	**GGBBB (g-4)**	**GBBBB (b-7)**	**BBBBB (b-6)**
	GGGBG (g-4)	**GGBGB (g-4)**	**GBGBB (g-5)**	**BGBBB (b-7)**	
	GGBGG (g-4)	**GBGGB (g-5)**	**GBBGB (g-6)**	**BBGBB (b-7)**	
	GBGGG (g-5)	**BGGGB (g-5)**	**GBBBG (g-7)**	**BBBGB (b-7)**	
	BGGGG (g-5)	**GGBBG (g-4)**	**BGGBB (g-5)**	**BBBBG (b-6)**	
		GBGBG (g-5)	**BGBGB (g-6)**		
		BGGBG (g-5)	**BGBBG (g-7)**		
		GBBGG (g-6)	**BBGGB (g-6)**		
		BGBGG (g-6)	**BBGBG (g-7)**		
		BBGGG (g-6)	**BBBGG (g-7)**		

TEACHER ACTION	TEACHER TALK	EXPECTED RESPONSE
Explain.	**Now we can count to find an answer to the two probability questions.**	
	How many of the 32 possible series would the Giraffes win?	26
	What is the P(G) (probability that the Giraffes win)?	$\frac{26}{32}$
	How many of the series would the Bears win?	6
	What is P(B)?	$\frac{6}{32}$

TEACHER ACTION	TEACHER TALK	EXPECTED RESPONSE
Explain.	The concessions manager is concerned about how many hotdogs he has on hand. If the series is likely to end quickly he does not want to have many extra hotdogs left over.	Students usually answer yes.
Ask.	Do you think the series is more likely to end in four games or in seven games?	Various answers.
Ask.	What do you think the probability is that the series will end in four games? We'll write this P(4).	Various answers.
	What do you think P(5) is? What do you think P(6) is? What do you think P(7) is?	Various answers.
	What do you think P(3) is?	Impossible; at least four games are needed.
Direct.	Let's go back through the list and count the lengths of each possible series. What are they?	Number of games ending in 4 games is 8. Number of games ending in 5 games is 8. Number of games ending in 6 games is 8. Number of games ending in 7 games is 8. Number of games ending in 3 games is 0.
	Now that we have our data analyzed we can count and answer the probability questions.	
	What is P(4)?	$P(4) = \frac{8}{32}$
	What is P(5)?	$P(5) = \frac{8}{32}$
	What is P(6)?	$P(6) = \frac{8}{32}$
	What is P(7)?	$P(7) = \frac{8}{32}$
	Are you surprised?	Usually students find this result amazing.
	What does this say to the concessions manager?	Various answers.

TEACHER ACTION	TEACHER TALK	EXPECTED RESPONSE
As an extra challenge or as homework, have students do a complete analysis of the situation where three games have already been played and the Giraffes have won two and the Bears one. Find P(G), P(B), P(4), P(5), P(6), P(7).		
Have fun with this one. Give students a tongue-in-cheek challenge.	You have done such a good job on the probability, it is time to let you show me how much you have learned. Put your name on a piece of paper and number it from 1 to 5. I have prepared five true-false questions on probability as a quiz for you. I'll read you the questions. Let's see where did I put them . . .	

The students' work should look like the following:

GGGG (g-5)	GGGB (g-5)	GGBB (g-5)	GBBB (b-7)	BBBB (b-6)
	GGBG (g-5)	GBGB (g-6)	BGBB (b-7)	
	GBGG (g-6)	BGGB (g-6)	BBGB (b-7)	
	BGGG (g-6)	GBBG (g-7)	BBBG (b-6)	
		BGBG (g-7)		
		BBGG (g-7)		

$P(G) = \frac{11}{16}$ $\quad P(4) = 0$

$P(B) = \frac{5}{16}$ $\quad P(5) = \frac{4}{16} = \frac{1}{4}$

$P(6) = \frac{6}{16} = \frac{3}{8}$

$P(7) = \frac{6}{16} = \frac{3}{8}$

TEACHER ACTION	TEACHER TALK	EXPECTED RESPONSE
Search around through your papers or the top of your desk.	I seem to have left them at home! Oh, well, no matter! Go ahead and take the test anyway. Do your best. Just guess what you think the answers are.	Various answers; T/F. Name 1. 2. 3. 4. 5.
Students will be puzzled, but encourage them to go ahead and guess the five answers.		
When everyone has written their five guesses, say.	Because I made a mistake and forgot to bring the quiz, I'll be very generous. Number from 1 to 5 and take the test over again.	Name (Example) 1. T 1. F 2. F 2. T 3. T 3. T 4. T 4. F 5. F 5. T
Direct.	Exchange papers with your neighbor and let's correct them. Because I cannot remember the questions, I'll flip a coin to determine the correct answers. Heads is true and tails is false.	
Flip a coin five times and call out correct answers. Example: H — "T is the correct answer." H — "T is the correct answer." T — "F is the correct answer." H — "T is the correct answer." T — "F is the correct answer."		

TEACHER ACTION	TEACHER TALK	EXPECTED RESPONSE
One student's paper might look like this: Name 1. T C 1. F X 2. F X 2. T C 3. T X 3. T X 4. T C 4. F X 5. F C 5. T X 3 correct 1 correct 2 wrong 4 wrong		
Direct.	Mark the number correct and the number wrong under each line of answers and pass the papers back to whomever they belong.	
Ask.	Did anyone have a perfect score on either try?	Various answers.
	Did anyone get them *all* wrong?	Various answers.
	How about 80% correct? That would be 4 correct, 1 wrong.	Various answers.
	How about 20% correct? That would be 1 correct, 4 wrong.	Various answers.
	How about 60% correct? That would be 3 correct, 2 wrong.	Various answers.
Explain.	Let's count these precisely and record the number of times each result happened.	
Record on the board or overhead: 5 correct – 0 wrong 4 correct – 1 wrong 3 correct – 2 wrong 2 correct – 3 wrong 1 correct – 4 wrong 0 correct – 5 wrong	Raise one hand if you got the result once; raise both hands if you got it twice. Then I can just count hands.	

TEACHER ACTION	TEACHER TALK	EXPECTED RESPONSE
Call out the list from top down; count results; record class numbers.		
Ask.	According to our class trials, what is the probability of guessing and getting the following results:	

Scores	Number of Students	Probability $\left(\frac{\text{Number of students}}{\text{Total number of tests}}\right)$
5 correct – 0 wrong		
4 correct – 1 wrong		
3 correct – 2 wrong		
2 correct – 3 wrong		
1 correct – 4 wrong		
0 correct – 5 wrong		

TEACHER ACTION	TEACHER TALK	EXPECTED RESPONSE
Ask.	How could we analyze this problem and find the exact probabilities?	Use the Smithville problem.
	Explain how we could use the Smith family's list.	Let the Gs be correct and the Bs be wrong.
Ask.	Then what is P(5C – 0W)?	$\frac{1}{32}$
	What is P(4C – 1W)?	$\frac{5}{32}$
	What is P(3C – 2W)?	$\frac{10}{32}$
	What is P(2C – 3W)?	$\frac{10}{32}$
	What is P(1C – 4W)?	$\frac{5}{32}$
	What is P(0C – 5W)?	$\frac{1}{32}$

TEACHER ACTION	TEACHER TALK	EXPECTED RESPONSE
	What is the probability of guessing and getting a score of 60% or better (three correct or better)?	$\frac{1 + 5 + 10}{32}$
	What is the probability of guessing and getting a score of 20% or better?	$\frac{1 + 5}{32}$
	Let's compute your long-term average, or expected value, if you take all your Five-Item True-False Tests by guessing.	
	What payoffs are possible on a Five-Item True-False Test if we grade on the basis of 100 points?	100, 80, 60, 40, 20, 0
	If you take 32 exams by guessing, how many times would you expect to score 100?	1
	How many times will you expect to score 80?	5
	How many times will you expect to score 60?	10
	How many times will you expect to score 40?	10
	How many times will you expect to score 20?	5
	How many times will you expect to score 0?	1
	This would give you how many total points on the 32 exams?	$1 \times 100 = 100$ $5 \times 80 = 400$ $10 \times 60 = 600$ $10 \times 40 = 400$ $5 \times 20 = 100$ $1 \times 10 = 0$ So the sum is 1600.

TEACHER ACTION	TEACHER TALK	EXPECTED RESPONSE
As you discuss the average scores, relate these percentages to the scoring system used in your classroom or school.	What would be your *average* for the 32 exams?	$\frac{1600}{32} = 50$
	Look like guessing is not a very good way to pass a course!	
Ask.	The situation was different for you because you got to take the test twice. Did anyone use the strategy on the second try of just reversing the answers?	Usually some students try this and expect the strategy to give at least one perfect paper.
Ask.	Does this strategy guarantee that one of the papers will be perfect?	No.
	Why?	Because if you have a pair of answers, one correct and one wrong on the first test they will be reversed on the second test, so that neither can be perfect.
	Think about this one. What is the worst score you can get if you use this strategy and get to keep the better of your two scores?	
Give students time to think. Record the answers offered. Call on some students who give the correct answer of 60% to give an explanation.		The possible pairs of tests are Best Score 5C – 0C 100% 4C – 1C 80% 3C – 2C 60% 2C – 3C 60% 1C – 4C 80% 0C – 5C 100%
As an extra challenge, ask.	What is the probability that you score 0% on a true-false test with six items if you guess each answer?	That would give $2 \times 2 \times 2 \times 2 \times 2 \times 2$ possibilities or 64. This gives $\frac{1}{64} = .0155 = .02$

TEACHER ACTION	TEACHER TALK	EXPECTED RESPONSE
Explain.	In the Smith families, the World Series, and the True-False Test we were dealing with events that have only two possibilities, boy-girl, win-lose, correct-wrong; and each possibility has an equally likely chance of occurring. Heads-Tails on a coin is also this sort of situation. These are called *binomial* situations. The prefix *bi* means two as in *bi*cycle (2 wheels). In this case, *bi*nomial means two possibilities.	
Pass out Worksheet 10-1, Pascal's Triangle. Display a transparency of Worksheet 10-1.	Let's think of some simple cases, such as the Smith families.	
Ask.	Suppose the families had only one child. What are the possibilities?	Girl or Boy G or B
Record on the overhead or the board: 1 1	I am going to make a pattern out of the answers we get. This will mean one way to get a G and one way to get a B.	
	If a family had two children, what would the possibilities be?	GG GB BB BG
Continue on the overhead or the board: 1 1 1 2 1	We'll record this as 1-2-1, meaning there is one way to get two girls, two ways to get one girl and one boy, and one way to get two boys.	
	What about three children? This will be 1-3-3-1.	GGG GGB GBB BBB GBG BGB BGG BBG
Add the row. 1 1 1 2 1 1 3 3 1	Fill in these three rows on your triangle.	

TEACHER ACTION	**TEACHER TALK**	**EXPECTED RESPONSE**
Fill in row 5. 1 1 Row 1 1 2 1 Row 2 1 3 3 1 Row 3 — — — — — Row 4 1 5 10 10 5 1 Row 5	We know what the results are for the fifth row (five children or five true-false questions). Let's fill it in.	
	Can you guess what row 4 is?	Various answers.
Record the correct response for row 4. Give hints: What is the first and last number? What is the second number, etc. Encourage students to look for patterns and symmetry. 1 4 6 4 1 Row 4		
Give the class time to struggle with row 6 for a bit. Some students may see how to find these numbers from the pattern so far.		
	I am going to give you a few minutes, working with a partner, to generate the numbers for the next three rows in the triangle pattern.	

TEACHER ACTION	TEACHER TALK	EXPECTED RESPONSE
Display Worksheet 10-1, Pascal's Triangle.	Let's look at the pattern you have generated. It's called Pascal's Triangle after the famous mathematician who first worked with the triangle.	1 1 1 2 1 1 3 3 1 1 4 6 4 1 1 5 10 10 5 1
Fill in rows 6, 7, and 8 on the overhead. Collect answers from the class.	Did you all have the first eight rows completed?	Various answers.
	Did anyone get the sixth row?	They will see that it begins with 1, 6 and ends with 6, 1. Help them see that the 15, 20, 15 in the center came from the 5 + 10, 10 = 10, and 10 + 5 in the row above.
Ask.	Can we generate the seventh row by adding the two numbers above it?	Yes. 1 6 15 20 15 6 1 1 7 21 35 35 21 7 1
	Let's find the sum of all the numbers in each row.	
	What's the sum in row 1? What's the sum in row 2? What's the sum in row 3? What's the sum in row 4? What's the sum in row 5? What's the sum in row 6?	2 4 8 16 32 64
	What do you predict the sum will be in row 7?	128
	What will it be in row 8?	256
	What do we do to get the sum in the next row?	Double the sum, or multiply by 2.

TEACHER ACTION	TEACHER TALK	EXPECTED RESPONSE
Ask.	How can we use Pascal's Triangle to find out how many ways a family of seven children could include five girls?	
It might help to write the outcomes below row 7:	What row in the triangle describes all possible seven child families?	Row 7.
1 7 21 35 35 21 7 1	What are the numbers in row 7?	1 7 21 35 35 21 7 1
7G 6G 5G 4G 3G 2G 1G 0G 0B 1B 2B 3B 4B 5B 6B 7B	What does the first number tell us?	That there is only one way to include seven girls (or seven boys). The first and last numbers are always 1.
	What does the second number tell us?	That there are seven ways to have six girls, one boy (or six boys and one girl). This number also tells us how many children we have or how many times we are flipping a coin, etc.
	What does the third number tell us?	It tells that there are 21 ways to include five girls, two boys (or five boys and two girls).
	This is the answer to the question we started with. There are 21 ways that a family of seven children can include five girls.	
	How do we express the *probability* that a family of seven children will have five girls?	There are 128 possibilities in all (the sum of the row). This gives the probability of five girls in a family of seven: $\frac{21}{128} \approx .16.$
Assign Worksheet 10-2, using Pascal's Triangle. Page 2 of Worksheet 10-2 is harder and can be used as an extra challenge. It might help to work one or two problems in class to make sure the students can use the triangle correctly. You may want to have students discover other patterns in the triangle.	Here is a sheet with some questions that can be answered using Pascal's Triangle.	

NAME

Pascal's Triangle

Total

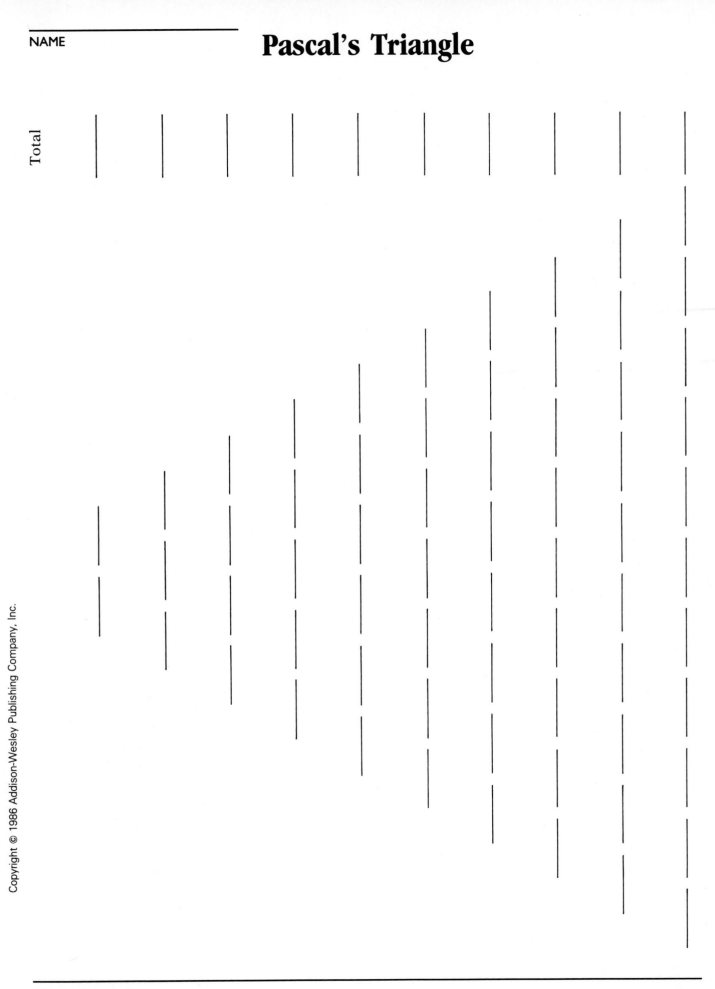

NAME ______________________

Using Pascal's Triangle

For each question, copy the row of Pascal's Triangle that will help you find the answer.

1. A coin is tossed six times. What is the probability that exactly three heads and three tails occurred?

_____ _____ _____ _____ _____ _____ _____ ‖ _____ Total

2. On a five-question true-false test, what is the probability that you will guess exactly two correct?

3. On a nine-question true-false test, what is the probability that you will guess exactly three correct?

4. A coin is tossed six times. What is the probability that *at least* two heads occur?

5. On a five-question true-false test, what is the probability that you will guess at least four correct?

Use the spinner below to answer questions 6 and 7.

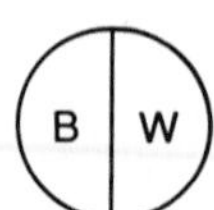

6. If the spinner is spun six times, what is the probability that exactly two spins will land on W?

7. What is the probability that a spinner spun eight times will land on B at least four times?

NAME

Using Pascal's Triangle

8. What will be the sum of the 20th row of the triangle?

9. What is the probability that a die tossed 20 times will land on an odd number at most one time?

10. Which is greater, A or B?

A is the probability of tossing seven coins and getting two or three heads.

B is the probability of tossing eight coins and getting exactly five heads.

11. What is the probability that a Smithville family picked at random will be the family GGBGB?

12. What is the probability that a Smithville family will have three girls and two boys?

13. Remember the paper carrier, Sue? A customer owes her \$5 per week for the paper. The customer offers her the following deals. Find the expected value of each and decide which is fair in the long run.

Toss five coins. If they land four or more heads the customer pays \$9. Otherwise he pays \$2.

Toss five coins. If they land all the same the customer pays \$40. Otherwise he pays \$2.

NAME ______________

Review Problems

Answer each of the following.

1. A bag contains two red, three white, and four blue marbles.

a. What is the probability of drawing a red marble? ________.

What is the probability of drawing a white marble? ________.

What is the probability of drawing a blue marble? ________.

b. Find the sum: P(R) + R(W) + P(B) = ________.

c. What is the probability of not drawing a blue marble? ________.

What is the probability of not drawing a blue or a red marble? ________.

2. Repeat problem 1, doubling the number of each color marble.

How does this affect the probabilities?

3. Repeat problem 1, adding one of each color marble to the bag.

How does this affect the probabilities?

4. Three chips are tossed. The red chip has a side A and a side B. The yellow chip has a side B and a side C. The blue chip has both sides marked A.

a. Use a tree diagram to find all the possible outcomes.

b. Find the probability of getting exactly

one C	________	one B	________	one A	________
two Cs	________	two Bs	________	two As	________

c. Player I scores a point if a pair of As turn up, and player II scores a point if a pair of Bs or a C turns up.

What is the probability of each player scoring?

Change the game to make it fair.

NAME ____________________

Review Problems

5. Two dice are tossed. Find the probability of getting

a sum of 7 ____________ a product of 6 ____________

a sum of 2 or 12 ____________ a product of 1 or 36 ____________

an even sum ____________ a product less than 15 ____________

a sum less than 6 ____________ an odd product ____________

a sum which is a multiple of 5 ______ a product which is a multiple of 6 ______

6. If three dice are tossed, what is the probability of getting

a. three odd numbers?

b. two odd and one even number?

c. at most one odd number?

7. Use the spinner below to answer 7a and 7b.

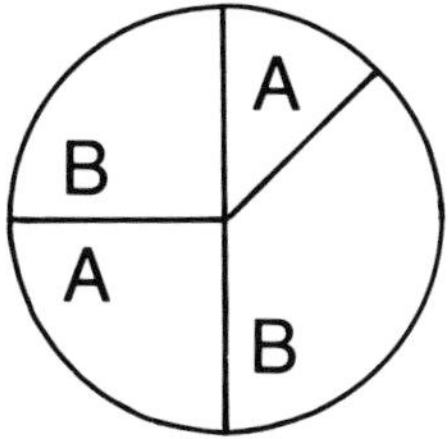

a. What is the probability the spinner will land on A? ____________

What is the probability the spinner will land on B? ____________

b. What is the probability the spinner will land on A two times in a row? ____________

8. A basketball player has a 70% free throw shooting average. The player goes up for a one-and-one free throw situation.

a. What is the probability the player will score

0 points? ____________ 1 point? ____________ 2 points? ____________

b. What is the average number of points the player can expect to make over the long run? ____________

NAME ______________________

Review Problems

9. You are offered the following choices for a weekly allowance:

$6 a week, or the amount of money you select by drawing two bills from a bag containing one $10 bill and four $1 bills.

a. How much money could you expect to average per week over the long run if you select to draw out of the bag each week?

b. Which plan would you choose?

10. In the maze below, John will pick a path at random. Use the grid to find

the probability that John will enter room A. ______________

the probability that John will enter room B. ______________

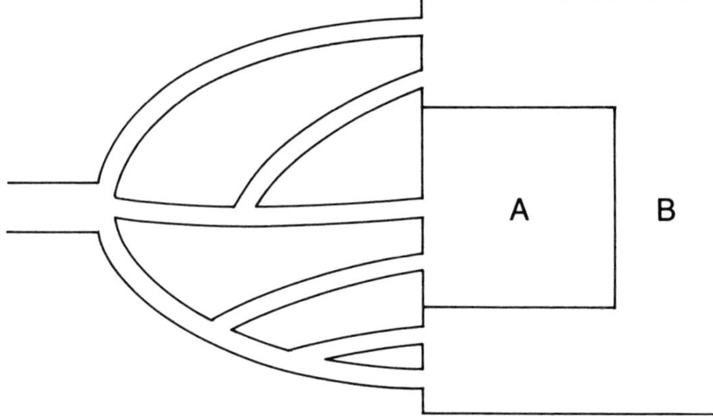

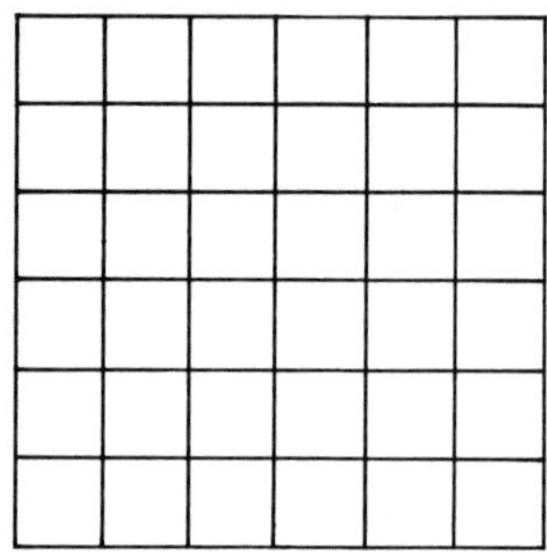

11. On a four-question true-false test on which you guess the answers, what is the probability of getting

a. a perfect paper (100%)? ______________

b. exactly 2 wrong? ______________

c. at most 1 wrong? ______________

NAME ____________________

Review Problems

12. Six pennies are flipped. What is the probability of getting

a. two heads and four tails? ____________

b. four heads and two tails? ____________

c. at least three heads? ____________

d. at most two tails? ____________

13. A bag contains one red marble and one white marble. Marbles are drawn and replaced in a bag before the next draw.

a. What is the probability that a red marble will be drawn two times in a row?

b. In ten draws, what is the probability that a red marble will be drawn at least five times?

14. In a survey of 50 students on their favorite sandwich, the results are

Peanut Butter	32
Ham and Cheese	10
Chicken Salad	7
Liverwurst	1

a. If a student is picked at random at the school, what is the probability that the student favors chicken salad or peanut butter?

b. If there are 500 students in the school, how many would you expect to favor peanut butter?

NAME ____________________

Unit Test

Choose the best answer to each question.

1. A spinner is divided into 15 sections of equal size. Five of these sections are red, four are blue, three are green, and three are yellow. If the spinner is spun, what is the probability that it will stop on a blue section?

A $\frac{1}{3}$ B $\frac{4}{15}$ C $\frac{4}{11}$ D $\frac{11}{15}$ E 4

2. The probability of an event happening is $\frac{3}{8}$. What is the probability that the event will *not* happen?

A 0 B $\frac{3}{8}$ C $\frac{5}{8}$ D $\frac{3}{4}$ E 1

3. A bowl contains three red marbles, five green marbles, and four blue marbles. A blue marble is drawn and not replaced. Then the contents of the bowl are thoroughly mixed. After this, you are asked to draw a marble from the bowl without looking. What is the probability that you will draw a blue marble?

A $\frac{3}{12}$ B $\frac{3}{11}$ C 12 D $\frac{4}{11}$ E $\frac{1}{3}$

4. Which of the following numbers could *not* be a probability?

A 1 B $\frac{3}{7}$ C $\frac{8}{9}$ D $\frac{5}{4}$ E 0

5. A coin has been tossed ten times and has come up heads each time. Which of the following statements is *true?*

A The coin will come up heads on the next toss.

B The coin will come up tails on the next toss.

C There is an equal chance of coming up heads or tails on the next toss.

D The coin is more likely to come up heads on the next toss.

E The coin is more likely to come up tails on the next toss.

6. What is the probability of getting exactly one head and one tail when two fair coins are tossed?

A $\frac{1}{4}$ B $\frac{1}{3}$ C 1 D $\frac{2}{3}$ E $\frac{1}{2}$

NAME ______________________

Unit Test

7. If two dice are tossed over and over again, which sum would you expect to occur most often?

A 6 B 7 C 8 D 9 E 12

8. What is the probability of getting a sum of 12 when two dice are thrown?

A $\frac{1}{2}$ B $\frac{1}{3}$ C $\frac{1}{6}$ D $\frac{1}{12}$ E $\frac{1}{36}$

9. Bill Bailey tossed a thumbtack 50 times. It landed point up 22 times. If he tossed the same thumbtack 250 times, about how many times would you expect it to land point up?

A 88 B 110 C 125 D 200 E 250

Questions 10–12 relate to the five spinners shown below.

I

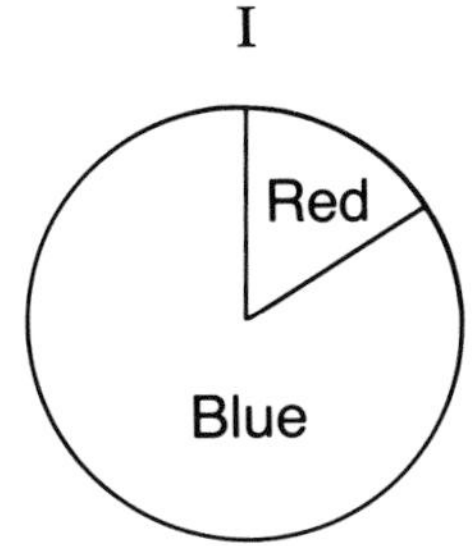

II

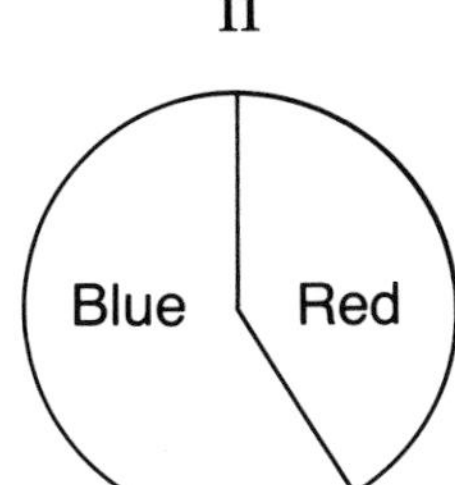

III

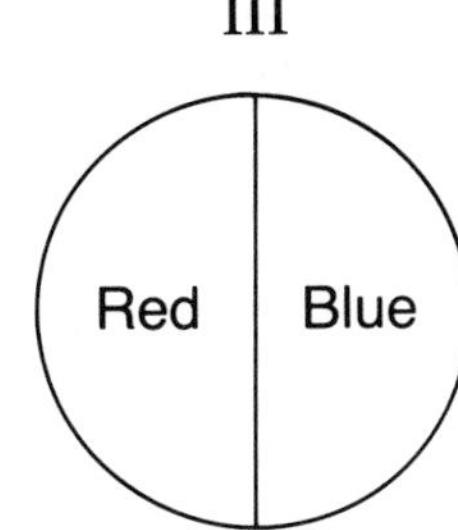

IV

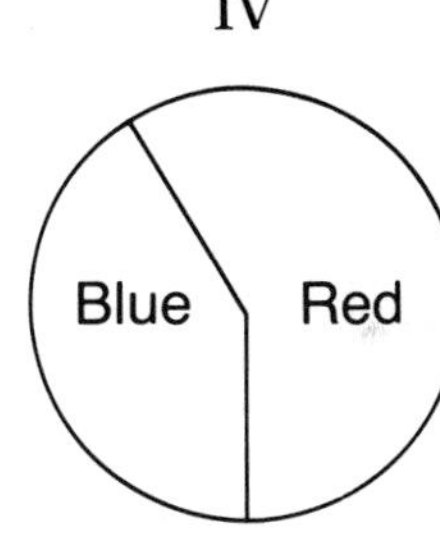

V

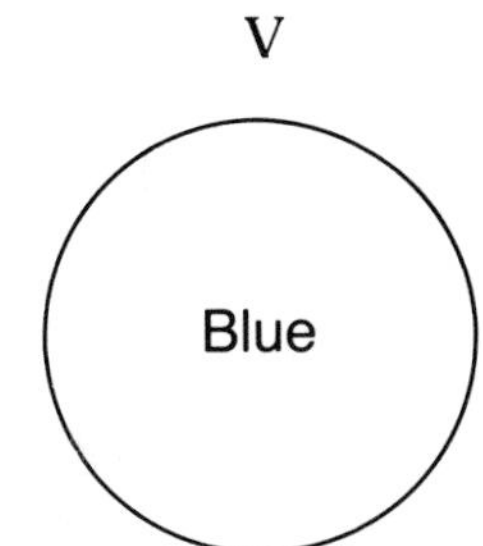

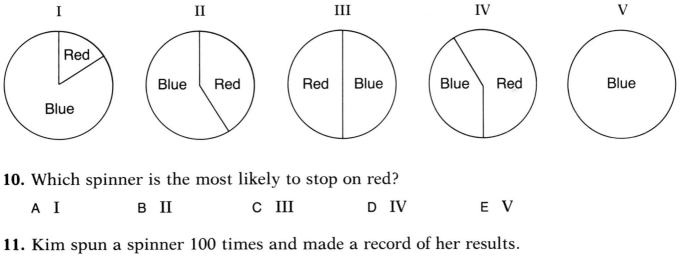

10. Which spinner is the most likely to stop on red?

A I B II C III D IV E V

11. Kim spun a spinner 100 times and made a record of her results.

Outcome	Blue	Red
Number of times	86	14

Which spinner is most likely the one Kim used?

A I B II C III D IV E V

12. If spinner III is spun twice, what is the probability of getting red both spins?

A $\frac{1}{4}$ B $\frac{1}{2}$ C $\frac{1}{8}$ D $\frac{3}{4}$ E 1

NAME ______________________

Unit Test

13. A bag contains only red and blue marbles. The probability of drawing a red marble is $\frac{3}{5}$. What is the probability of drawing a blue marble?

A $\frac{5}{3}$ B $\frac{1}{5}$ C $\frac{2}{5}$ D $\frac{3}{5}$ E 1

14. A bag contains two yellow, two blue, and four red marbles. How many blue marbles must be added to the bag to make the probability of drawing a blue marble $\frac{1}{2}$?

A 1 B 2 C 3 D 4 E None

15. Three pennies are tossed. What is the probability of getting two heads and one tail?

A $\frac{1}{8}$ B $\frac{1}{3}$ C $\frac{2}{3}$ D $\frac{1}{2}$ E $\frac{3}{8}$

16. John is tossing bean bags randomly onto the mat below. What is the probability of a bean bag landing in an area marked B?

A
A
B
B
B
B

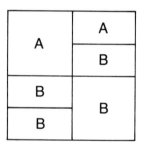

A $\frac{1}{4}$ B $\frac{3}{8}$ C $\frac{1}{2}$ D $\frac{5}{8}$ E $\frac{2}{3}$

17. Sally has a 50% free throw shooting average in basketball. She goes to the line to take two shots. What is the probability that she will make both shots?

A $\frac{1}{4}$ B $\frac{1}{2}$ C $\frac{1}{8}$ D $\frac{3}{4}$ E 1

NAME ______________________

Unit Test

18. Hat 1 and Hat 2 contain red and white marbles, as shown below. A hat is chosen at random and a marble is drawn from it.

Hat 1

W
W R

Hat 2

Which area model can be used to find the probability of drawing a white marble?

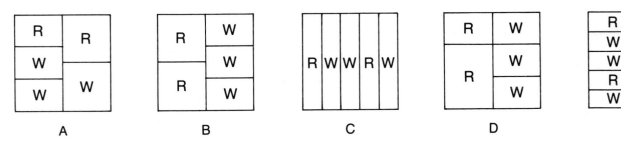

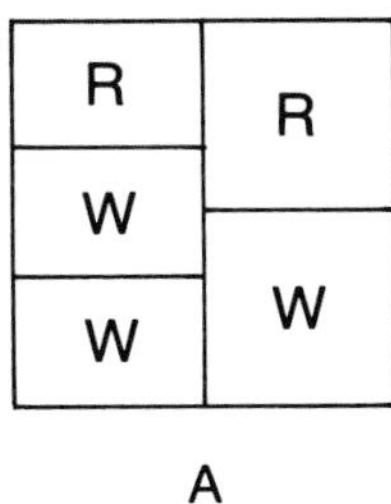

A

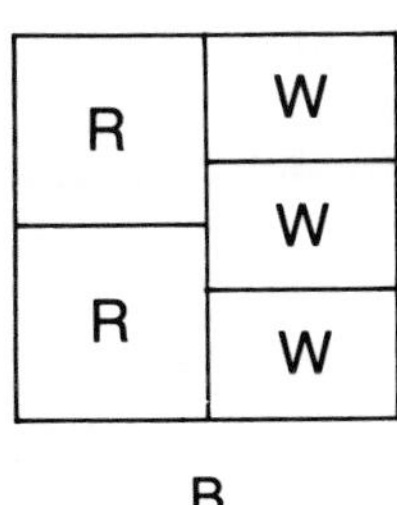

B

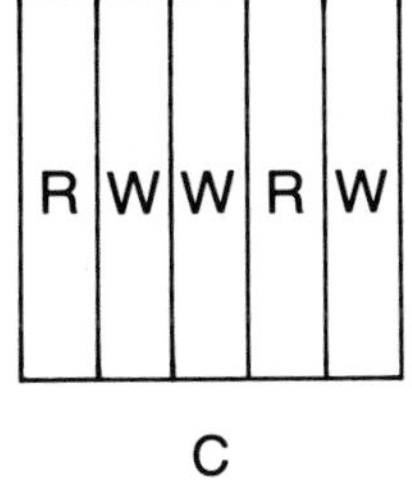

C

R W
R W
W

D

R R
W W
W W
R R
W W

E

19. Bag 1 and Bag 2 contain blocks, as shown below.

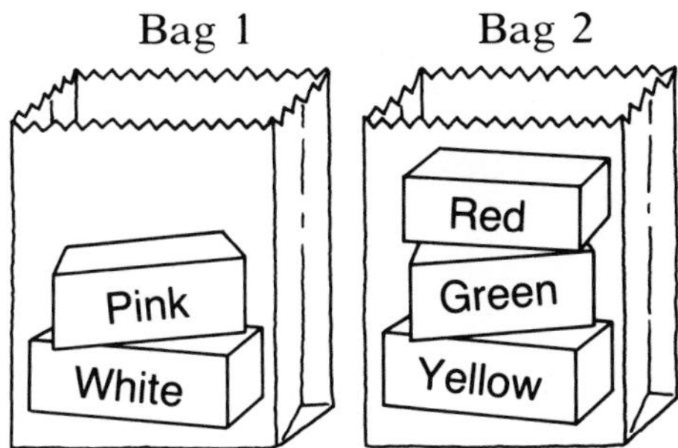

Which of the following is a tree diagram showing the possible combined results of drawing a block from Bag 1, and then a block from Bag 2?

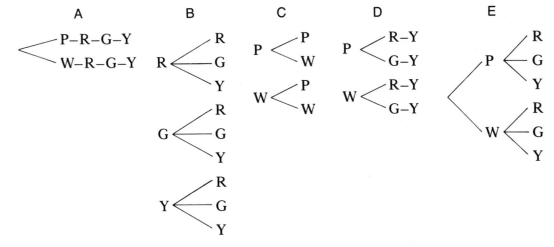

A

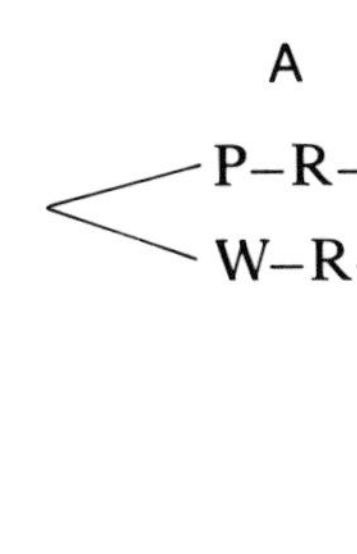

B

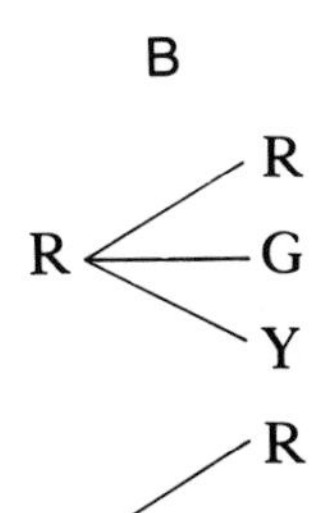

C

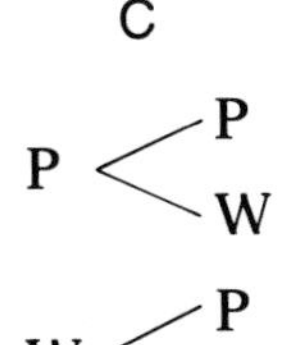

D

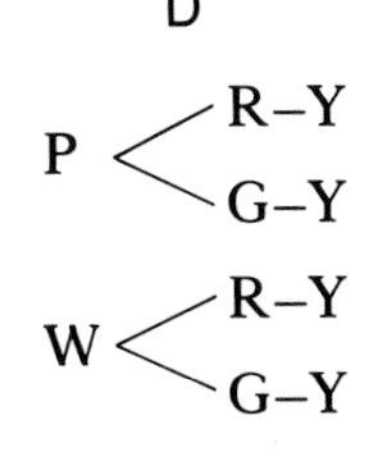

E

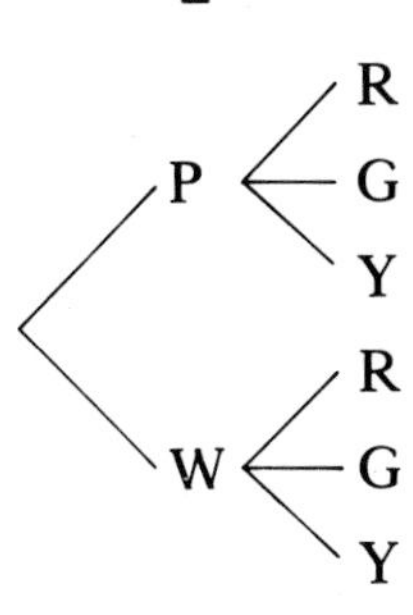

NAME ______________________

Unit Test

20. Two coins are flipped. Player A gets a point if the coins match, and player B gets a point if there is no match. In this game

A A is more likely to win

B B is more likely to win.

C A and B have the same chances of winning.

D There is not enough information to decide.

E B can never win.

21. Two bills are drawn from a bag containing a five-dollar bill and three one-dollar bills. If the experiment is repeated many times, what would you expect the average amount of money drawn per time to be?

A \$2 B \$3 C \$4 D \$5 E \$6

22. What is the probability that a family of three children will have two girls and one boy?

A $\frac{1}{8}$ B $\frac{1}{3}$ C $\frac{2}{3}$ D $\frac{1}{2}$ E $\frac{3}{8}$

23. How many different ways could you answer a four-item true-false test?

A 1 B 2 C 4 D 8 E 16

Questions 24 and 25 relate to the information given below. In order to determine what ice cream flavors to have in the cafeteria, a random poll is taken of 30 students on their favorite flavor. The results are:

Vanilla	8	Strawberry	5	Peppermint	3
Chocolate	10	Butter Pecan	4		

24. If there are 600 students in the school, about how many would you expect to prefer chocolate?

A 10 B 20 C 200 D 250 E 300

25. If a student is chosen at random, what is the probability that the student favors either chocolate or butter pecan?

A $\frac{10}{30}$ B $\frac{14}{30}$ C $\frac{4}{30}$ D $\frac{6}{30}$ E $\frac{16}{30}$

NAME ______________________

Unit Test Answer Sheet

1. A B C D E
2. A B C D E
3. A B C D E
4. A B C D E
5. A B C D E

6. A B C D E
7. A B C D E
8. A B C D E
9. A B C D E
10. A B C D E

11. A B C D E
12. A B C D E
13. A B C D E
14. A B C D E
15. A B C D E

16. A B C D E
17. A B C D E
18. A B C D E
19. A B C D E
20. A B C D E

21. A B C D E
22. A B C D E
23. A B C D E
24. A B C D E
25. A B C D E

NAME ____________

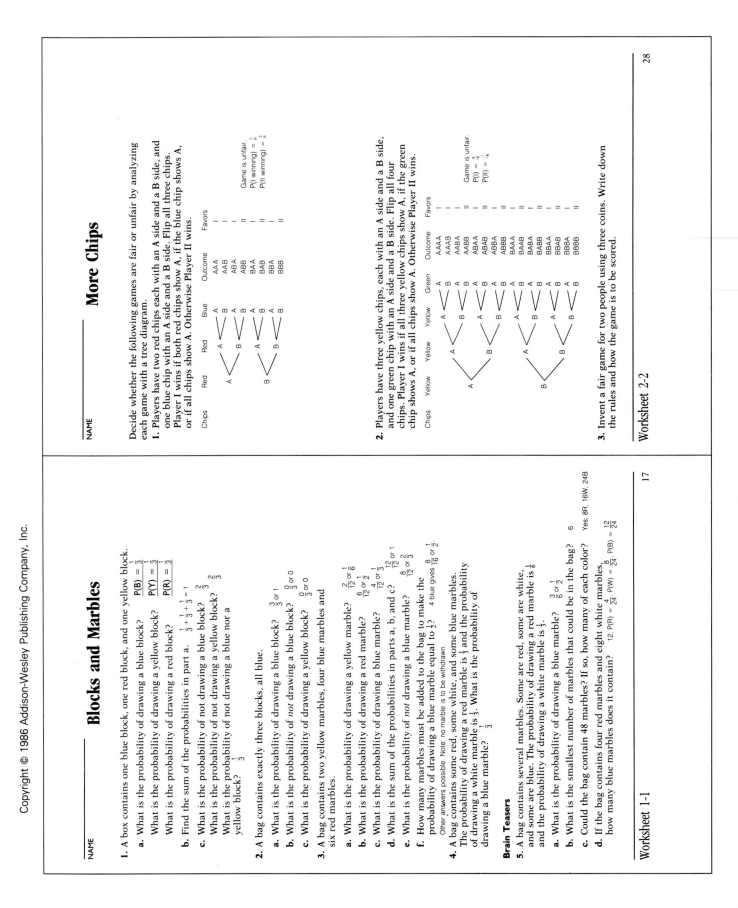

Blocks and Marbles

1. A box contains one blue block, one red block, and one yellow block.
   a. What is the probability of drawing a blue block? $P(B) = \frac{1}{3}$
      What is the probability of drawing a yellow block? $P(Y) = \frac{1}{3}$
      What is the probability of drawing a red block? $P(R) = \frac{1}{3}$
   b. Find the sum of the probabilities in part a. $\frac{1}{3} + \frac{1}{3} + \frac{1}{3} = 1$
   c. What is the probability of not drawing a blue block? $\frac{2}{3}$
      What is the probability of not drawing a yellow block? $\frac{2}{3}$
      What is the probability of not drawing a blue nor a yellow block? $\frac{1}{3}$
2. A bag contains exactly three blocks, all blue.
   a. What is the probability of drawing a blue block? $\frac{3}{3}$ or 1
   b. What is the probability of *not* drawing a blue block? $\frac{0}{3}$ or 0
   c. What is the probability of drawing a yellow block? $\frac{0}{3}$ or 0
3. A bag contains two yellow marbles, four blue marbles and six red marbles.
   a. What is the probability of drawing a yellow marble? $\frac{2}{12}$ or $\frac{1}{6}$
   b. What is the probability of drawing a red marble? $\frac{6}{12}$ or $\frac{1}{2}$
   c. What is the probability of drawing a blue marble? $\frac{4}{12}$ or $\frac{1}{3}$
   d. What is the sum of the probabilities in parts a, b, and c? $\frac{12}{12}$ or 1
   e. What is the probability of *not* drawing a blue marble? $\frac{8}{12}$ or $\frac{2}{3}$
   f. How many marbles must be added to the bag to make the probability of drawing a blue marble equal to $\frac{1}{2}$? 4 blue gives $\frac{8}{16}$ or $\frac{1}{2}$.
      Other answers possible. Note: no marble is to be withdrawn.
4. A bag contains some red, some white, and some blue marbles. The probability of drawing a red marble is $\frac{1}{3}$ and the probability of drawing a white marble is $\frac{1}{3}$. What is the probability of drawing a blue marble? $\frac{1}{3}$

Brain Teasers

5. A bag contains several marbles. Some are red, some are white, and some are blue. The probability of drawing a red marble is $\frac{1}{6}$ and the probability of drawing a white marble is $\frac{1}{3}$.
   a. What is the probability of drawing a blue marble? $\frac{3}{6}$ or $\frac{1}{2}$
   b. What is the smallest number of marbles that could be in the bag? 6
   c. Could the bag contain 48 marbles? If so, how many of each color? Yes; 8R, 16W, 24B
   d. If the bag contains four red marbles and eight white marbles, how many blue marbles does it contain? 12; $P(R) = \frac{4}{24}$, $P(W) = \frac{8}{24}$, $P(B) = \frac{12}{24}$

NAME ____________

More Chips

Decide whether the following games are fair or unfair by analyzing each game with a tree diagram.

1. **Players have two red chips each with an A side and a B side, and one blue chip with an A side and a B side. Flip all three chips. Player I wins if both red chips show A, if the blue chip shows A, or if all chips show A. Otherwise Player II wins.**

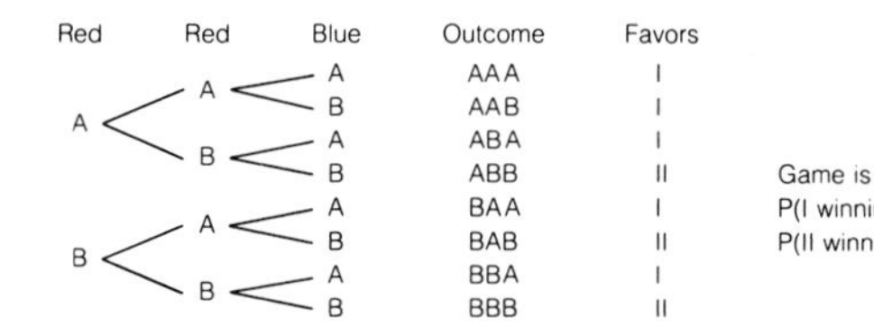

Game is unfair.
P(I winning) = $\frac{5}{8}$
P(II winning) = $\frac{3}{8}$

2. **Players have three yellow chips, each with an A side and a B side, and one green chip with an A side and a B side. Flip all four chips. Player I wins if all three yellow chips show A, if the green chip shows A, or if all chips show A. Otherwise Player II wins.**

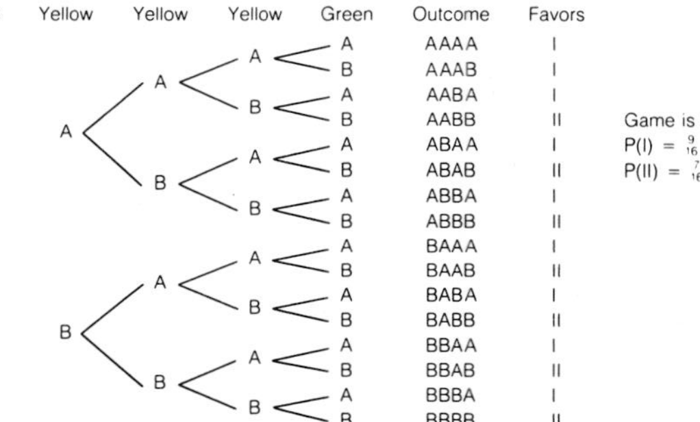

Game is unfair.
P(I) = $\frac{9}{16}$
P(II) = $\frac{7}{16}$

3. **Invent a fair game for two people using three coins. Write down the rules and how the game is to be scored.**

NAME

Analyzing Two-Dice Games

Game I
Sum

	1	2	3	4	5	6
1	2	3	4	5	6	7
2	3	4	5	6	7	8
3	4	5	6	7	8	9
4	5	6	7	8	9	10
5	6	7	8	9	10	11
6	7	8	9	10	11	12

Total sums = 36

Total number of even sums = 18

Total number of odd sums = 18

P (even sum) = $\frac{18}{36}$ or $\frac{1}{2}$

P (odd sum) = $\frac{18}{36}$ or $\frac{1}{2}$

Game 2
Product

	1	2	3	4	5	6
1	1	2	3	4	5	6
2	2	4	6	8	10	12
3	3	6	9	12	15	18
4	4	8	12	16	20	24
5	5	10	15	20	25	30
6	6	12	18	24	30	36

Total products = 36

Total number of even products = 27

Total number of odd products = 9

P (even product) = $\frac{27}{36}$ or $\frac{3}{4}$

P (odd product) = $\frac{9}{36}$ or $\frac{1}{4}$

NAME

More Dice Games

1. A pair of dice are tossed. Find the probability of getting
   - A sum of 3 $\frac{2}{36}$ or $\frac{1}{18}$
   - A sum of 9 $\frac{4}{36}$ or $\frac{1}{9}$
   - A sum greater than 7 $\frac{15}{36}$
   - A sum which is a multiple of 3 $\frac{12}{36}$ or $\frac{1}{3}$
   - A sum which is a multiple of 4 $\frac{9}{36}$ or $\frac{1}{4}$
   - A product of 12 $\frac{4}{36}$ or $\frac{1}{9}$
   - A product greater than 12 $\frac{13}{26}$
   - A product less than 12 $\frac{19}{36}$
   - A product that is a multiple of 5 $\frac{11}{36}$
   - A product that is a multiple of 3 or 4 $\frac{28}{36}$ or $\frac{7}{9}$

Decide whether games 3 and 4 are fair or unfair. If unfair, who has the advantage? Describe a way to assign points to make it fair.

Game 3

Toss two dice. Subtract the smaller number from the larger number. Player I scores one point if the difference is odd. Player II scores one point if the difference is even. (Note: Zero is an even number.)

	1	2	3	4	5	6
1	0	1	2	3	4	5
2	1	0	1	2	3	4
3	2	1	0	1	2	3
4	3	2	1	0	1	2
5	4	3	2	1	0	1
6	5	4	3	2	1	0

P(odd) = $\frac{18}{36}$ or $\frac{1}{2}$

P(even) = $\frac{18}{36}$ or $\frac{1}{2}$

Game is fair.

Game 4

Toss two dice. Find the product.
Player I scores one point if the product is a multiple of 4.
Player II scores one point if the product is a multiple of 3.

Refer to product table to count number of multiples of 4 and 3.

P(multiple of 4) = $\frac{15}{36}$

P(multiple of 3) = $\frac{20}{36}$

Game is unfair. To make fair, give Player I 20 points per score and Player II 15 points per score.

NAME ______________

Spinners

For each spinner, determine the probability of the indicated regions.

1. Spin 100 times.

	Tally	Total
A		
B		

P(A) = ______

P(B) = ______

2. Spin 100 times.

	Tally	Total
A		
B		
C		
D		

P(A) = ______ P(C) = ______

P(B) = ______ P(D) = ______

3. Spin 100 times.

	Tally	Total
A		
B		
C		
D		

P(A) = ______ P(C) = ______

P(B) = ______ P(D) = ______

NAME ______________

Experimental Probabilities

1. Select a passage from a book. Count the number of vowels and the total number of letters in the passage. Tabulate your results in the table below.

Vowel	Number Counted	P
a		
e		
i		
o		
u		
Total Letters in the Passage		

Use this probability to predict the number of e's in another passage. Check the passage to see how close your prediction comes to the actual count.

2. A poll was taken of 40 students on their favorite school lunch. The results are below.

Hamburgers and fries	14
Pizza and salad	13
Spaghetti and salad	8
Hot dogs and beans	5
Liver and spinach	0
Total	40

a. If a student is chosen at random, what is the probability that he or she favors

Hamburgers and fries? $\frac{14}{40}$
Pizza and salad? $\frac{13}{40}$
Spaghetti and salad? $\frac{8}{40}$
Hot dogs and beans? $\frac{5}{40}$
Liver and spinach? 0

b. If there are 400 students in the school, how many prefer

Hamburgers? 140 Hot dogs? 50 Liver? 0

c. How can the cook use this information to plan a menu for 20 school days?

7 days for hamburgers; 6 or 7 days for pizza; 4 days for spaghetti; and 2 or 3 days for hot dogs.

NAME

Experimental Probabilities

3. A poll is taken of 50 students on their opinions of a rule that would prohibit them from riding bikes to school. The results of the poll are tabulated below.

	Students who ride to school on a bike	Students who ride to school in a bus	Students who walk to school	Total
Favor the Rule	1	12	10	23
Oppose the Rule	8	10	4	22
No Opinion	1	3	1	5
Total	10	25	15	50

If a student is chosen at random, what is the probability that he or she

favors the rule? $\frac{23}{50}$
rides a bus and opposes the rule? $\frac{10}{50}$
rides a bike or opposes the rule? $\frac{1+8+1+10+4}{50} = \frac{24}{50}$

4. It has been estimated that in using a calculator, a mistake is made once in every 25 entries. If a certain problem requires 75 entries on the calculator, what is the probability that an error is made? $\frac{3}{75}$

What is the probability that no error is made? $\frac{72}{75}$

5. Conduct a poll in your class on one of the following items. Check it with a sample of students outside of your class.
   a. What is the favorite color?
   b. What is the favorite song?
   c. What day of the week has the most absences? (Check results of this one with the school office.)
   d. Is tardiness related to distance from school? Break students into groups of bus riders, car riders, one block walkers, two block walkers, etc.

NAME

Which Is Best?

You are given two hats, two white marbles, and two red marbles. Which arrangement of the two white and two red marbles in the hats gives the best chance of drawing a white marble?

H1 (W, R) H2 (W, R)

$P(W) = \frac{1}{2}$
$P(R) = \frac{1}{2}$

H1 (W, W) H2 (R, R)

$P(W) = \frac{1}{2}$
$P(R) = \frac{1}{2}$

H1 (R) H2 (W, W, R)

$P(W) = \frac{12}{36}$ or $\frac{1}{3}$
$P(R) = \frac{24}{36}$ or $\frac{2}{3}$

H1 (W) H2 (W, R, R)

$P(W) = \frac{24}{36}$ or $\frac{2}{3}$
$P(R) = \frac{12}{36}$ or $\frac{1}{3}$

H1 ( ) H2 (R, W, R, W)

$P(W) = \frac{1}{4}$
$P(R) = \frac{1}{4}$

Note: Squares must be split to partition the total area into four congruent parts.

Note: No marbles in Hat 1.

NAME ______

Darts, Anyone?

1. Pat and Erin are playing a game with the board shown at the right. A dart is thrown at random at the board. Pat scores a point if the dart lands in an area marked A. Erin scores a point if the dart lands in an area marked B. Is this a fair game? No

   P(A) = $\frac{9}{16}$ P(B) = $\frac{7}{16}$

2. Find probabilities for this board. Would this board make a fair dart game? No

   P(A) = $\frac{14}{32}$ P(B) = $\frac{18}{32}$

3. If a dart is thrown at random at this dart board, what is the probability that it will land in area A? What is the probability it will land in area B? What is the probability it will land in area C?

   P(A) = $\frac{16}{25}$ P(B) = $\frac{8}{25}$ P(C) = $\frac{1}{25}$

   Scoring: If a dart landing in A scores one point, how many points should a dart landing in C score to make the two areas yield the same number of points over the long run? What should a dart in area B score?

   Points for C 16 Points for B 2

4. What is the probability that a dart thrown at random at this board will land in area A? What is the probability it will land in area B?

   P(A) = $\frac{7}{16}$ P(B) = $\frac{9}{16}$

   How would you assign points so that the game would be fair?

   Points for A 9 Points for B 7

NAME ______

Darts, Anyone?

5. In the space below design a path for the story about Mr. Green and the students. Use the grid to analyze your path. Find the room in which the students should place the cookbook.

B

A

6. Jane used this grid to analyze a probability problem.

   What probabilities should be assigned to A, B, and C?

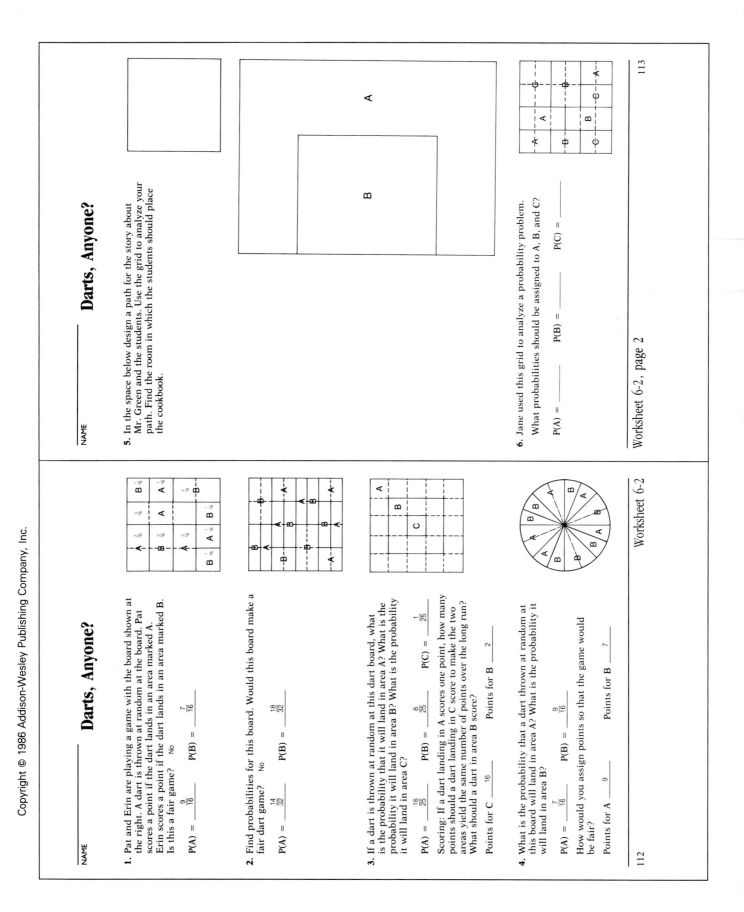

   P(A) = ______ P(B) = ______ P(C) = ______

NAME

One-And-One Basketball Shots

60% Shooter (60% = $\frac{60}{100}$ or $\frac{6}{10}$)

P(0) = $\frac{40}{100}$

P(1) = $\frac{24}{100}$

P(2) = $\frac{36}{100}$

Most likely outcome 0 points.

Average points per trip ______.
$\frac{96}{100}$ or .96 points

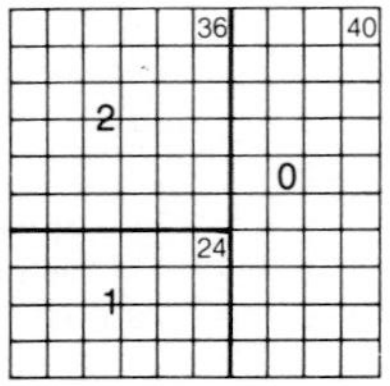

40% Shooter (40% = $\frac{40}{100}$ or $\frac{4}{10}$)

P(0) = $\frac{60}{100}$

P(1) = $\frac{24}{100}$

P(2) = $\frac{16}{100}$

Most likey outcome 0 points.

Average points per trip ______.
$\frac{56}{100}$ or .56 points

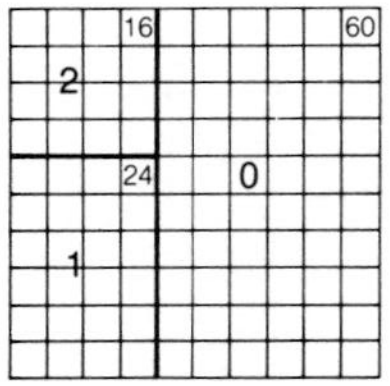

20% Shooter

P(0) = $\frac{80}{100}$

P(1) = $\frac{16}{100}$

P(2) = $\frac{4}{100}$

Most likely outcome 0 points.

Average points per trip ______.
$\frac{24}{100}$ or .24 points

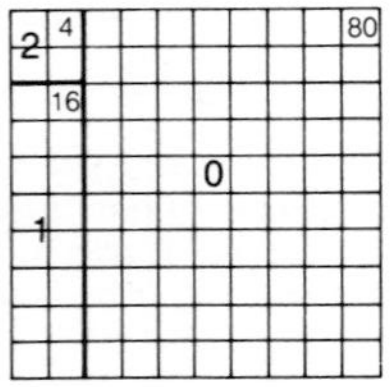

80% Shooter

P(0) = $\frac{20}{100}$

P(1) = $\frac{16}{100}$

P(2) = $\frac{64}{100}$

Most likely outcome 2 points.

Average points per trip ______.
$\frac{144}{100}$ or 1.44 points

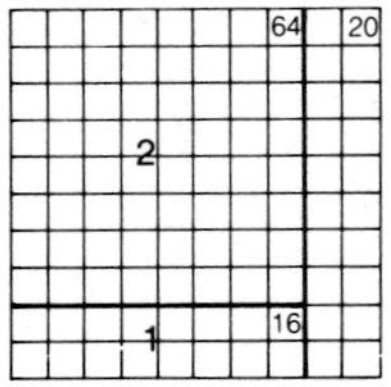

Fill in the chart and circle the most likely outcome for each shooter.

Summary

Shooter's Probability	Probability 0 points	1 point	2 points	Average points per trip
$\frac{2}{10}$	$\frac{80}{100}$	$\frac{16}{100}$	$\frac{4}{100}$	.24
$\frac{4}{10}$	$\frac{60}{100}$	$\frac{24}{100}$	$\frac{16}{100}$	.56
$\frac{6}{10}$	$\frac{40}{100}$	$\frac{24}{100}$	$\frac{36}{100}$	.96
$\frac{8}{10}$	$\frac{20}{100}$	$\frac{16}{100}$	$\frac{64}{100}$	

NAME

Newspaper Pay

In each of the following situations, the customer should pay \$5 per week for newspapers. Sue, the paper carrier, has to decide which of the schemes of chance would give her a fair deal over the long run. In each case, decide what Sue should do—accept or reject the proposal.

1. The customer will place a five-dollar bill and 3 one-dollar bills in a bag. Sue will draw out two bills.

FO_1 O_1O_2 O_2O_3 P(\$6) = $\frac{3}{6} = \frac{1}{2}$ E.V. (1 × \$6) + (1 × \$2) = \$8 total for 2 weeks.
FO_2 O_1O_3 P(\$2) = $\frac{3}{6} = \frac{1}{2}$
FO_3 $\frac{\$8}{2}$ = \$4 REJECT

2. The customer will place a five-dollar bill and 2 one-dollar bills in a bag. Sue will draw out two bills.

FO_1 O_1O_2 P(\$6) = $\frac{2}{3}$ E.V. (2 × \$6) + (1 × \$2) = \$14 total for 3 weeks
FO_2 P(\$2) = $\frac{1}{3}$ $\frac{\$14}{3}$ = \$4$\frac{2}{3}$ REJECT

3. Sue will toss three coins. If two or more land heads, Sue gets \$9. Otherwise, she gets \$1.

HHH HHT HTT TTT P(2 or more H) = $\frac{1}{2}$
HTH THT P(otherwise) = $\frac{1}{2}$
THH TTH E.V. (1 × \$9) + (1 × \$1) = \$10 total for 2 weeks.
$\frac{\$10}{2}$ = 5 ACCEPT

4. Sue will toss three coins. If all land the same, all heads or all tails, Sue gets \$15. Otherwise, she gets \$1.

P(All same) = $\frac{2}{8} = \frac{1}{4}$ E.V. (1 × \$15) + (3 × \$1) = \$18 total for 4 weeks.
P(otherwise) = $\frac{6}{8} = \frac{3}{4}$ $\frac{\$18}{4}$ = \$4.50 REJECT

5. Sue rolls a pair of dice. If the sum is exactly 7, Sue gets \$20. Otherwise she gets \$2.

P(Sum 7) = $\frac{6}{36} = \frac{1}{6}$ E.V. (1 × \$20) + (5 × \$2) = \$30 total for 6 weeks.
P(otherwise) = $\frac{30}{36} = \frac{5}{6}$ $\frac{\$30}{6}$ = \$5 ACCEPT

6. Sue will roll a pair of dice. If the sum is at most 4, Sue will get \$20. What should she get otherwise to make the payoff fair in the long run?

P(Sum 2, 3, or 4) = $\frac{6}{36} = \frac{1}{6}$
P(otherwise) = $\frac{30}{36} = \frac{5}{6}$

To make the payoff fair in the long run, Sue must average \$5 × 6 = \$30 for every 6 weeks.
(1 × \$20) + (5 × \$□) = \$30
□ = \$2 gives \$30 for 6 weeks and makes E.V. = \$5.

NAME

Pascal's Triangle

											Total
1	1										2
1	2	1									4
1	3	3	1								8
1	4	6	4	1							16
1	5	10	10	5	1						32
1	6	15	20	15	6	1					64
1	7	21	35	35	21	7	1				128
1	8	28	56	70	56	28	8	1			256
1	9	36	84	126	126	84	36	9	1		512
1	10	45	120	210	252	210	120	45	10	1	1024

Worksheet 10-1 167

NAME

Using Pascal's Triangle

For each question, copy the row of Pascal's Triangle that will help you find the answer.

1. A coin is tossed six times. What is the probability that exactly three heads and three tails occurred?

1	6	15	20	15	6	1	64
6H	5H1T	4H2T	3H3T				Total

P(3H3T) = $\frac{20}{64} = \frac{15}{16}$

2. On a five-question true-false test, what is the probability that you will guess exactly two correct?

1	5	10	10	5	1	32
0 correct	1 correct	2 correct				

P(2 correct) = $\frac{10}{32} = \frac{5}{16}$

3. On a nine-question true-false test, what is the probability that you will guess exactly three correct?

1	9	36	84	126	126	84	36	9	1	512
0 correct	1 correct	2 correct	3 correct							

P(3 correct) = $\frac{84}{512} = \frac{21}{128}$

4. A coin is tossed six times. What is the probability that *at least* two heads occur?

1	6	15	20	15	6	1	64
0H6T	1H5T	2H4T	3H3T	4H2T	5H1T	6H0T	

P(at least 2 heads) = $\frac{15 + 20 + 15 + 6 + 1}{64} = \frac{57}{64}$

5. On a five-question true-false test, what is the probability that you will guest at least four correct?

1	5	10	10	5	1	32
5 correct	4 correct	3 correct				

P(at least 4 correct) = $\frac{1 + 5}{32} = \frac{6}{32} = \frac{3}{16}$

Use the spinner below to answer questions 6 and 7.

B | W

6. If the spinner is spun six times, what is the probability that exactly two spins will land on W?

1	6	15	20	15	6	1	64
0W6B	1W5B	2W4B					

P(2W) = $\frac{15}{64}$

7. What is the probability that a spinner spun eight times will land on B at least four times?

1	8	28	56	70	56	28	8	1	256
8B	7B	6B	5B	4B	3B	2B	1B	0B	

P(at least 4Bs) = $\frac{1 + 8 + 28 + 56 + 70}{256} = \frac{163}{256}$

168 Worksheet 10-2

NAME ____________

Using Pascal's Triangle

8. What will be the sum of the 20th row of the triangle?

$2^{20} = 1{,}048{,}576$

9. What is the probability that a die tossed 20 times will land on an odd number at most one time?

$\frac{20 + 1}{1{,}048{,}576} = \frac{21}{1{,}048{,}576}$

10. Which is greater, A or B?

A is the probability of tossing seven coins and getting two or three heads.

$\frac{21 + 35}{128} = \frac{56}{128} = \frac{7}{16}$

B is the probability of tossing eight coins and getting exactly five heads.

$\frac{56}{256} = \frac{7}{32}$

11. What is the probability that a Smithville family picked at random will be the family GGBGB?

$\frac{1}{32}$

12. What is the probability that a Smithville family will have three girls and two boys?

$\frac{10}{32}$

13. Remember the paper carrier, Sue? A customer owes her \$5 per week for the paper. The customer offers her the following deals. Find the expected value of each and decide which is fair in the long run.

Toss five coins. If they land four or more heads the customer pays \$9. Otherwise he pays \$2.

P(4 or 5 heads) $= \frac{6}{32}$ E.V. (6 × \$9) + (26 × \$2) = \$106

P(Otherwise) $= \frac{26}{32}$ $\frac{\$106}{32} \approx \$3.31$ UNFAIR

Toss five coins. If they land all the same the customer pays \$40. Otherwise he pays \$2.

P(All same) $= \frac{2}{32} = \frac{1}{16}$ E.V. (1 × \$40) + (15 × \$2) = \$70

P(Otherwise) $= \frac{30}{32} = \frac{15}{16}$ $\frac{\$70}{16} \approx \$4.38$ UNFAIR

NAME

Review Problems

Answer each of the following.

1. A bag contains two red, three white, and four blue marbles.

a. What is the probability of drawing a red marble? $\frac{2}{9}$.

What is the probability of drawing a white marble? $\frac{3}{9}$ or $\frac{1}{3}$.

What is the probability of drawing a blue marble? $\frac{4}{9}$.

b. Find the sum: P(R) + R(W) + P(B) = $\frac{9}{9}$ or 1.

c. What is the probability of not drawing a blue marble? $\frac{5}{9}$.

What is the probability of not drawing a blue or a red marble? $\frac{6}{9}$ or $\frac{2}{3}$.

2. Repeat problem 1, doubling the number of each color marble.

How does this affect the probabilities? They remain the same. $\frac{4}{18} = \frac{2}{9}; \frac{6}{18} = \frac{3}{9}; \frac{8}{18} = \frac{4}{9}$

3. Repeat problem 1, adding one of each color marble to the bag.

How does this affect the probabilities? Two are different. $\frac{3}{12}_{red} \neq \frac{2}{9}; \frac{5}{12}_{blue} \neq \frac{4}{9}$; but $\frac{4}{12}_{white} = \frac{3}{9}$

4. Three chips are tossed. The red chip has a side A and a side B. The yellow chip has a side B and a side C. The blue chip has both sides marked A.

a. Use a tree diagram to find all the possible outcomes.

b. Find the probability of getting exactly

one C $\frac{4}{8} = \frac{1}{2}$ one B $\frac{4}{8} = \frac{1}{2}$ one A $\frac{4}{8} = \frac{1}{2}$

two Cs $\frac{0}{8} = 0$ two Bs $\frac{2}{8} = \frac{1}{4}$ two As $\frac{4}{8} = \frac{1}{2}$

c. Player I scores a point if a pair of As turn up, and player II scores a point if a pair of Bs or a C turns up.

What is the probability of each player scoring?

P( ) = $\frac{1}{2}$ P( ) = $\frac{3}{4}$

Change the game to make it fair.

Let Player I score 3 points and Player II score 2 points when their respective situations occur.

A — B — A ABA
A — B — A ABA
A — C — A ACA
A — C — A ACA
B — B — A BBA
B — B — A BBA
B — C — A BCA
B — C — A BCA

NAME

Review Problems

5. Two dice are tossed. Find the probability of getting

a sum of 7 $\frac{6}{36}$ or $\frac{1}{6}$ a product of 6 $\frac{4}{36}$ or $\frac{1}{9}$

a sum of 2 or 12 $\frac{2}{36}$ or $\frac{1}{18}$ a product of 1 or 36 $\frac{2}{36}$ or $\frac{1}{18}$

an even sum $\frac{18}{36}$ or $\frac{1}{2}$ a product less than 15 $\frac{23}{36}$

a sum less than 6 $\frac{10}{36}$ or $\frac{5}{18}$ an odd product $\frac{9}{36}$

a sum which is a multiple of 5 $\frac{7}{36}$ a product which is a multiple of 6 $\frac{15}{36}$ or $\frac{5}{12}$

6. If three dice are tossed, what is the probability of getting

a. three odd numbers? $\frac{1}{8}$

b. two odd and one even number? $\frac{3}{8}$

c. at most one odd number? $\frac{1}{2}$

7. Use the spinner below to answer 7a and 7b.

B A B B B A A B

a. What is the probability the spinner will land on A? $\frac{3}{8}$

What is the probability the spinner will land on B? $\frac{5}{8}$

b. What is the probability the spinner will land on A two times in a row? $\frac{3}{8} \times \frac{3}{8} = \frac{9}{64}$

8. A basketball player has a 70% free throw shooting average. The player goes up for a one-and-one free throw situation.

a. What is the probability the player will score

0 points? $\frac{30}{100}$ 1 point? $\frac{7}{10} \times \frac{3}{10} = \frac{21}{100}$ 2 points? $\frac{7}{10} \times \frac{7}{10} = \frac{49}{100}$

b. What is the average number of points the player can expect to make over the long run? 1.19

NAME

Review Problems

9. You are offered the following choices for a weekly allowance:

$6 a week, or the amount of money you select by drawing two bills from a bag containing one $10 bill and four $1 bills.

a. How much money could you expect to average per week over the long run if you select to draw out of the bag each week?

$P(11) = \frac{4}{10}$ $P(2) = \frac{6}{10}$ $(4 \times 11) + (6 \times 2) = 44 + 12 = 56$ $\frac{\$56}{10} = \$5.60$

b. Which plan would you choose?

The $6 per week.

10. In the maze below, John will pick a path at random. Use the grid to find

the probability that John will enter room A. $P(A) = \frac{12}{36}$ or $\frac{1}{3}$

the probability that John will enter room B. $P(B) = \frac{24}{36}$ or $\frac{2}{3}$

A B

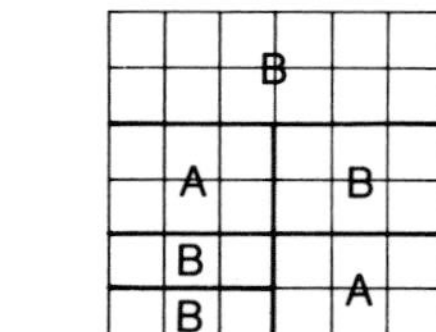

11. On a four-question true-false test on which you guess the answers, what is the probability of getting

a. a perfect paper (100%)? $\frac{1}{16}$

b. exactly 2 wrong? $\frac{6}{16}$ or $\frac{3}{8}$

c. at most 1 wrong? $\frac{5}{16}$

NAME

Review Problems

12. Six pennies are flipped. What is the probability of getting

a. two heads and four tails? $\frac{15}{64}$

b. four heads and two tails? $\frac{15}{64}$

c. at least three heads? $\frac{42}{64}$ or $\frac{21}{32}$

d. at most two tails? $\frac{22}{64}$ or $\frac{11}{32}$

13. A bag contains one red marble and one white marble. Marbles are drawn and replaced in a bag before the next draw.

a. What is the probability that a red marble will be drawn two times in a row?

$\frac{1}{2} \times \frac{1}{2} = \frac{1}{4}$

b. In ten draws, what is the probability that a red marble will be drawn at least five times?

$\frac{638}{1{,}024}$ or $\frac{319}{512}$

14. In a survey of 50 students on their favorite sandwich, the results are

Peanut Butter	32
Ham and Cheese	10
Chicken Salad	7
Liverwurst	1

a. If a student is picked at random at the school, what is the probability that the student favors chicken salad or peanut butter?

$\frac{39}{50}$

b. If there are 500 students in the school, how many would you expect to favor peanut butter?

$\frac{32}{50} \times 500 = 320$

Unit Test Answer Key

1. B
2. C
3. B
4. D
5. C

6. E
7. B
8. E
9. B
10. D

11. A
12. A
13. C
14. D
15. E

16. D
17. A
18. A
19. E
20. C

21. C
22. E
23. E
24. C
25. B